Designing with FPGAs and CPLDs

Bob Zeidman

CMP Books
Lawrence, Kansas 66046

CMP Books
CMP Media LLC
1601 West 23rd Street, Suite 200
Lawrence, Kansas 66046
USA
www.cmpbooks.com

The programs in this book are presented for instructional value. The programs have been carefully tested, but are not guaranteed for any particular purpose. The publisher does not offer any warranties and does not guarantee the accuracy, adequacy, or completeness of any information herein and is not responsible for any errors or omissions. The publisher assumes no liability for damages resulting from the use of the information in this book or for any infringement of the intellectual property rights of third parties that would result from the use of this information.

Acquisition Editor:	Robert Ward
Layout design & production:	Justin Fulmer and Michelle O'Neal
Managing Editor:	Michelle O'Neal
Cover art design:	Damien Castaneda

Distributed in the U.S. by:
Publishers Group West
1700 Fourth Street
Berkeley, California 94710
1-800-788-3123
www.pgw.com

Distributed in Canada by:
Jaguar Book Group
100 Armstrong Avenue
Georgetown, Ontario M6K 3E7 Canada
905-877-4483

Printed and bound in the United Kingdom

Transferred to Digital Printing, 2010

ISBN: 1-57820-112-8

CMP Books

This book is dedicated to two smart, dedicated, inspiring teachers who departed this world much too soon, but left a legacy of enthusiastic engineers, mathematicians, and scientists.

Mrs. Anita Field was my ninth grade teacher at George Washington High School in Philadelphia. She demonstrated to classes of restless, awkward, prepubescent boys and girls that math could be fun and exciting. She showed by her example that those who studied math could be cultured, well-rounded, and even pretty.

Mr. Gordon Stremlau was a human calculating machine with a dry sense of humor that we only understood when we were seniors at GWHS. What we first thought were snide remarks and nasty smirks, as freshman, we later came to realize were clever comments and inside jokes. It was only after some level of maturity that we could appreciate the subtlety of his wit.

Both of these people were mentors, and friends, and I wish that I had the opportunity to thank them personally. And though I'm saddened by the fact that there are few others like them, as dedicated and excited, teaching our children, there is some comfort in knowing that I and my friends have benefited from knowing them.

Table of Contents

Chapter 3   Field Programmable Gate Arrays (FPGAs) 33

Chapter 4   Universal Design Methodology for Programmable
Devices 55

Chapter 5   Design Techniques, Rules,
and Guidelines 73

Foreword

Design is a process whereby the designer realizes an embodiment of an objective or specification. Design is necessarily a selection among alternatives, usually many alternatives. The goal for the designer is to pick the "best" alternative. Usually designs are not unique. Many different designs can serve a common function. Indeed, there can be several "best" designs, each satisfying a different criterion: design effort, reliability, manufacturability, item cost, functional robustness, etc. Inferior designs are simply designs that on any criteria could have been better.

This book deals with a particular type of logical device design: programmable logic devices (or PLDs). Given the ongoing advance in electronics, these devices have grown significantly in capability and complexity. The two most interesting types of PLDs: C(complex)PLD and FPGA (field programmable gate arrays) are the focus of the book's interest. PLDs, being programmable, have the important capability of being re-configurable. They can be reprogrammed to rapidly realize another function. This valuable capability can easily seduce the unwary designer into a design trap. Quickly produce an inferior design with the intent on reconfiguring to a better design later. Unfortunately there may not be enough time or PLD flexibility to realize the better design.

This book is well aware of design pitfalls. The author, Bob Zeidman, has a special combination of talents: he's a well-known and experienced designer and he has the ability to see and explain the whole design process. His secrets for good design include planning ahead with a well thought out specification and through verification at each step of the design process. A special feature of the book is Bob's first hand design experience. He presents this through sidebars as personal notes and observations applied to particular design principles.

A really unique contribution of the book is contained in Chapter 4 — Universal Design Methodology for Programmable Devices. This Universal Design Methodology is a must read for any PLD designer. Following this methodology is probably the best way to avoid inferior PLD designs and insure working and reliable PLD systems. The methodology is based heavily on Bob's experience and is tailored here to PLD design issues. It's overall an important contribution to logic design.

Michael J. Flynn
Emeritus Professor of Electrical Engineering
Stanford University

Preface

Complex Programmable Logic Devices (CPLDs) and Field Programmable Gate Arrays (FPGAs) have become a critical part of every system design. The ability to test designs, fix bugs in the field, and adapt existing hardware to new protocols and standards is attractive to all electrical engineers. Unfortunately, this ability to speed up the design process by assuming that these devices can be fixed later is also attractive to many engineers and managers. This can lead to sloppy design and incomplete testing. One purpose of this book is to give you information on how to design programmable devices quickly yet thoroughly so that redesigns are needed only to add or change functionality, not to correct bugs.

Many vendors offer many different architectures and technologies for programmable devices. Which one is right for your design? How do you design a system so that it works correctly and functions as you expect in your entire system? How do you plan resources and prepare a schedule for the chip design? These are questions that this book sets out to answer.

Book Organization

The book is organized into eight chapters. If you're thorough and have a deep thirst for knowledge, you can read all of them. If you have a busy schedule, you can read only those chapters that pertain to your role in the project. In the following section, "Intended Audience," I give suggestions for those chapters that pertain to specific job functions.

Preface

This is the chapter you are now reading.

Chapter 1: Prehistory: Programmable Logic to ASICs

This chapter talks about the history of programmable devices before CPLDs and FPGAs and examines their benefits and limitations. It also discusses application specific integrated circuits (ASICs) built from uncommitted gate arrays. It provides an understanding of the basic technologies of programmable devices and the market forces that created a need for them. No detailed knowledge of electrical engineering is required for understanding this chapter, but it certainly helps.

Chapter 2: Complex Programmable Logic Devices (CPLDs)

This chapter deals with the internal architecture of CPLDs and the semiconductor technologies upon which they are based. The basic architectural blocks are examined in detail. I assume that the reader has a basic understanding of electronics and digital circuit design.

Chapter 3: Field Programmable Gate Arrays (FPGAs)

This chapter deals with the internal architecture of FPGAs and the semiconductor technologies upon which they are based. The basic architectural blocks are examined in detail. I assume that the reader has a basic understanding of electronics and digital circuit design.

Chapter 4: Universal Design Methodology for Programmable Devices

This chapter presents a design methodology for creating fully functional, reliable chips. It includes a design flow for a CPLD-based or FPGA-based project that conforms to this methodology. This chapter describes all of the phases of the design that need to be planned, allowing a designer or project manager to allocate resources and create a schedule. You need no particular knowledge of engineering to understand this chapter.

Chapter 5: Design Techniques, Rules, and Guidelines

This chapter examines in detail the issues that arise when designing a circuit that is to be implemented in a CPLD or FPGA. These are detailed technical issues and require at least an undergraduate level knowledge of electronics and digital circuit design. The concepts presented in this chapter are essential to designing a chip that functions correctly in your system and will be reliable throughout the lifetime of your product.

Chapter 6: Verification

This chapter examines in detail the issues that arise when verifying the correctness of a CPLD or FPGA design. The chapter focuses on designing for testability and how to exhaustively simulate your design. The issues examined are detailed technical issues and require at least an undergraduate level knowledge of electronics and digital circuit design. The concepts presented in this chapter are essential to designing a chip that functions correctly in your system and will be reliable throughout the lifetime of your product.

Chapter 7: Electronic Design Automation Tools

In this chapter I discuss the various tools used for CPLD and FPGA design. The functionality of each kind of tool is examined, including the variations from various EDA tool vendors. I assume that the reader has a basic understanding of electronics and digital circuit design.

Chapter 8: Today and the Future

The final chapter discusses new types of programmable devices, new uses for programmable devices, and hybrid devices that combine aspects of programmability with aspects of ASICs. Technical knowledge is helpful for reading this chapter, but in-depth knowledge of engineering is not needed.

Appendix A: Answer Key

Here you can find all of the answers to the questions at the end of each chapter. Wouldn't it be great if life were this easy?

Appendix B: Verilog Code for Schematics in Chapter 5

This section contains the Verilog code for many of the schematics that appear in figures in Chapter 5. Each schematic is identified and the corresponding code is given.

Glossary

This section contains definitions of important words, terms, acronyms, and abbreviations used throughout the book.

References

This section contains useful books and websites for further information about the topics covered in this book.

Intended Audience

This book can be read by different people for different purposes. Engineers who are designing their first circuit to be implemented in a programmable device will find that the book provides great guidelines for the entire process. Experienced engineers will find tips and techniques that will speed up the design process and give them a better chance for a working, reliable design. Engineering managers will gain an understanding of the design process and will be in a better position to schedule a CPLD or FPGA design and plan the necessary resources for it. Sales and Marketing personnel will find the book useful for gaining a broad understanding of programmable devices.

Although I hope that you'll have the time to read the book from cover to cover for it's great wealth of information, I realize that you may not have the time. Here are my suggestions if you're going to skip around.

• Design Engineers

I suggest that design engineers read Chapters 2 through 4 to gain the technical understanding needed before attempting a design. Chapter 8 will give you an understanding of newer technologies that are just now becoming available.

• Engineering Project Leaders

I suggest that project leaders read Chapters 2 through 4. These chapters will enable you to understand the technology and also plan the resources and create a realistic schedule. Chapter 4, which covers the Universal Design Methodology, will give you a good understanding of the overall design process. Chapter 8 will give you an understanding of newer technologies that are just now becoming available.

• Managers

Managers will find Chapter 4 on the Universal Design Methodology to be the most useful. This will enable you to plan the resources and create a realistic schedule.

• Sales and Marketing

People employed in Sales and Marketing will find Chapter 1 helpful for understanding the market need that CPLDs and FPGAs have filled. Chapters 2 and 3 will be useful for understanding the basic technology of the various devices from different manufacturers, and their advantages and trade-offs. Chapter 8 will give you some insight into current state of the art as well as into technologies down the road.

Content

I have created this book from my years of experience designing not only CPLDs and FPGAs, but digital design of all kinds including ASICs, printed circuit boards, and systems. Each chapter contains practical information for planning, creating, programming, testing, and maintaining a programmable device.

In my attempt to make this book useful and relevant, I have included diagrams, code samples, and practical examples wherever possible. The diagrams are labeled, the code is documented, and the examples are explained in detail.

Exercises

In order to reinforce the concepts, there are exercises at the end of each chapter. Obviously, it is up to you to determine whether to take the quizzes — I won't be grading you — but I think completing the quizzes will make the concepts stick better in your mind. In this way, the quizzes are designed as learning tools. The Answer Key begins on page 173.

"Depth Control" — Sidebars and Notes

A unique aspect of this book is the concept of "Depth Control," where additional content is included to help clarify or illustrate the concepts being discussed or to simply add to your knowledge in general. Areas that fall into the category of Depth Control are presented in sidebars throughout the book. Often this material consists of detailed technical information relating to the topic. This technical information is more in-depth than you need, or is not essential for understanding the topic, but you may find it interesting. Also, I sometimes use these sidebars to give personal observations or relate personal experiences that are relevant to the material being discussed. You can skip these sections without missing any of the most important concepts, but I think that these diversions not only make the subject more interesting, they can give it a real-world perspective.

Support and Feedback

I welcome your comments. I've made a good effort to check the correctness of the book and the exercises at the end of each chapter. Other people have double-checked my work. Of course, there's still a possibility that something got by. If you find any mistakes or have suggestions for improvements, please contact me.

Acknowledgments

As they say, no man is an island, no great thing is created suddenly, nobody knows the trouble I've seen, and no book is the work of only one person. With that in mind, I'd like to acknowledge and thank those people who helped, shaped, pushed, prodded, annoyed, cajoled, and assisted with this book.

First is Robert Ward, Editor, at CMP Books. Robert, thanks for your encouragement and assistance in making this a much easier effort. And thanks for your rigorous review of the manuscript and excellent suggestions for modifications and additions.

Next I'd like to thank the entire staff at Chalkboard who has been patient with me and supportive of my extra-curricular literary efforts.

Many people provided insight and information and took the time to fill out my online surveys about FPGA design and FPGA tools. I'd like to thank the following people for their input, in reverse alphabetical order: Doug Warmke, Carlo Treves, John Tobey, Bob Slee, Dan Pugh, Chris Phillips, Jonathan Parlan, Sam Ochi, Ghulam Nurie, Charlie Neuhauser, Ike Nassi, Jay Michlin, Ken McElvain, Joe McAlexander, Lance Leventhal, Brian Jackman, Faisal Haque, Dan Hafeman, Miguel Gomez, Jason Feinsmith, Nader Fathi, Steve Eliscu, Brian Dipert, Giovanni De Micheli, Mitch Dale, Donald Cramb, Mike Breen, Pawan Agrawal, and Vishal Abrol.

I'd particularly like to thank Mike Flynn who graciously took the time to write the foreword and, more importantly, has encouraged me, and actually joined me, in many of my endeavors.

Finally, I'd like to thank my wife, Carrie, because she'd be annoyed if I didn't mention her. Mainly she'd be annoyed because she helped so much with the graphics in the book. And, of course, she put up with one more project of mine that went from idea to obsession

Bob Zeidman
Cupertino, California
Bob@ZeidmanConsulting.com
www.ZeidmanConsulting.com

Chapter 1

Prehistory: Programmable Logic to ASICs

Programmable devices have progressed through a long evolution to reach the complexity today to support an entire system on a chip (SOC). This chapter gives an approximately chronological discussion of these devices from least complex to most complex. I say "approximately" because there is definitely overlap between the various devices, which are still in use today. The chapter includes a discussion on application specific integrated circuits (ASICs) and how CPLDs and FPGAs fit within the spectrum of programmable logic and ASICs.

Objectives

The objectives of this chapter are to become aware of the different programmable devices available and how they led to the current state-of-the-art device. These objectives are summarized here:

- Learn the history of programmable devices.
- Obtain a basic knowledge of the technologies of programmable devices.
- Understand the architectures of earlier programmable devices.
- Discover the speed, power, and density limitations of earlier programmable devices.

1

- Appreciate the needs that arose and that were not addressed by existing devices, and that created a market for CPLDs and FPGAs.

Note

The ROM cell

The basic diagram for a ROM cell containing a single bit of data is shown in Figure 1.1. The word line is turned on if the address into the chip includes this particular bit cell. The metal layer is used to program the data into the ROM during fabrication. In other words, if the metal layer mask has a connection between the transistor output and the data line, the bit is programmed as a zero. When the bit is addressed, the output will be pulled to a low voltage, a logical zero. If there is no connection, the data line will be pulled up by the resistor to a high voltage, a logical one.

1.1 Programmable Read Only Memories (PROMs)

The first field programmable devices were created as alternatives to expensive mask-programmed ROM. Storing code in a ROM was an expensive process that required the ROM vendor to create a unique semiconductor mask set for each customer. Changes to the code were impossible without creating a new mask set and fabricating a new chip. The lead time for making changes to the code and getting back a chip to test was far too long.

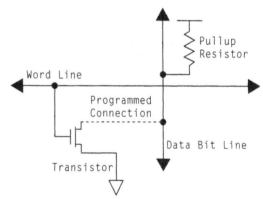

Figure 1.1   The ROM cell.

PROMs solved this problem by allowing the user, rather than the chip vendor, to store code in the device using a simple and relatively inexpensive desktop programmer. This new device was called a programmable read only memory (PROM). The process for storing the

Note

One-time programmable PROM cells

One-time programmable PROMs rely on an array of fuses and either diodes or transistors, as shown in Figure 1.2 and Figure 1.3. These fuses, like household fuses, consist of a wire that breaks connection when a large amount of current goes through it. To program a one-bit cell as a logic one or zero, the fuse for that cell is selectively burned out or left connected.

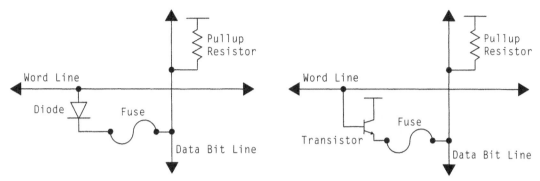

Figure 1.2   One-time programmable,
diode-based PROM cell

Figure 1.3   One-time programmable,
transistor-based PROM cell

code in the PROM is called programming, or "burning" the PROM. PROMs, like ROMs, retain their contents even after power has been turned off.

Although the PROMs were initially intended for storing code and constant data, design engineers also found them useful for implementing logic. The engineers could program state machine logic into a PROM, creating what is called "microcoded" state machines. They could easily change these state machines in order to fix bugs, test new functions, optimize existing designs, or make changes to systems that were already shipped and in the field.

Eventually, erasable PROMs were developed which allowed users to program, erase, and reprogram the devices using an inexpensive, desktop programmer. Typically, PROMs now refer to devices that cannot be erased after being programmed. Erasable PROMS include erasable programmable read only memories (EPROMs) that are programmed by applying high-voltage electrical signals and erased by flooding the devices with UV light. Electrically erasable programmable read only memories (EEPROMs) are programmed and erased by

---

Note _____

Reprogrammable PROM cells

Reprogrammable PROMs essentially trap electric charge on the input of a transistor that is not connected to anything. The input acts like a capacitor. The transistor amplifies the charge. During programming, the charge is injected onto the transistor by one of several methods, including *tunneling* and *avalanche injection*. This charge will eventually leak off. In other words, some electrons will gradually escape, but the leakage will not be noticeable for a long time, on the order of ten years, so that they remain programmed even after power has been turned off to the device. Programming one of these devices causes wear and tear on the chip while the electrons are being injected. Most devices can be programmed about 100,000 times before they begin to lose their capability to be programmed.

---

applying high voltages to the device. Flash EPROMs are programmed and erased electrically and have sections that can be erased electrically in a short time and independently of other sections within the device. For the rest of this chapter, I use the term PROM generically to refer to all of these devices unless I specifically state otherwise.

PROMs are excellent for implementing any kind of combinatorial logic with a limited number of inputs and outputs. Each output can be any combinatorial function of the inputs, no matter how complex. As I said, this isn't usually how engineers use PROMs in today's designs; they're used to hold bytes of data. However, if you look at Figure 1.4, you can see how each address bit for the PROM can be considered a logic input. Then, simply program each data output bit to have the value of the combinatorial function you are creating. Some early devices used PROMs in this way to create combinatorial logic.

For sequential logic, one must add external clocked devices such as flip-flops or micropro-cessors. A simplified example of a state machine built using a PROM is shown in Figure 1.5. The PROM is used to combine inputs with bits representing the current state of the machine, to produce outputs and the next state of the machine. This allows the creation of very complex state machines. Microcode is often decoded within a microprocessor using this method, where the microcode for control-ling the various stages of the microprocessor is stored in ROM.

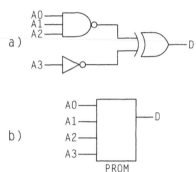

| Inputs | Output |
A[3:0]	D
0000	0
0001	0
0010	0
0011	0
0100	0
0101	0
0110	0
0111	1
1000	1
1001	1
1010	1
1011	1
1100	1
1101	1
1110	1
1111	0

Figure 1.4   a) combinatorial logic, b) equivalent PROM, c) logic values

The problem with PROMs is that they tend to be extremely slow — even today, access times are on the order of 40 nanosec-onds or more — so they are not useful for applications where speed is an issue. These days, speed is always an issue. Also, PROMs are not easily integrated into logic circuits on a chip because they require a different technology and therefore a different set of masks and processes than for logic circuits. Integrating PROMs

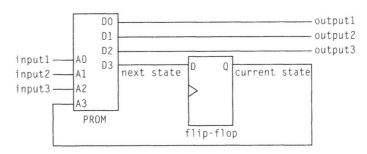

Figure 1.5 PROM-based state machine

onto a chip with logic circuitry involves extra masks and extra processing steps, all leading to extra costs.

1.2 Programmable Logic Arrays (PLAs)

Programmable logic arrays (PLAs) were a solution to the speed and input limitations of PROMs. PLAs consist of a large number of inputs connected to an AND plane, where different combinations of signals can be logically ANDed together according to how the part is programmed. The outputs of the AND plane go into an OR plane, where the terms are ORed together in different combinations and finally outputs are produced, as shown in Figure 1.6. At the inputs and outputs there are

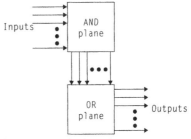

Figure 1.6 PLA architecture

inverters (not shown in the figure) so that logical NOTs can be obtained. These devices can implement a large number of combinatorial functions, but, unlike a PROM, they can't implement every possible mapping of their input set to their output set. However, they generally have many more inputs and are much faster.

As with PROMs, PLAs can be connected externally to flip-flops to create state machines, which are the essential building blocks for all control logic.

Each connection in the AND and OR planes of a PLA could be programmed to connect or disconnect. In other words, terms of Boolean equations could be created by selectively connecting wires within the AND and OR planes. Simple high level languages — ABEL, PALASM, and CUPL — were developed to convert Boolean equations into files that would program these connections within the PLA. These equations looked like this:

```
a = (b & !c) | (b & !d & e)
```

to represent the logic for

```
A = (B AND NOT C) OR (B & NOT D AND E)
```

This added a new dimension to programmable devices in that logic could now be described in readable programs at a level higher than ones and zeroes.

1.3 Programmable Array Logic (PALs)

The programmable array logic (PAL) is a variation of the PLA. Like the PLA, it has a wide, programmable AND plane for ANDing inputs together. The AND plane is shown by the crossing wires on the left in Figure 1.7. Programming elements at each intersection in the AND plane allow perpendicular traces to be connected or left open, creating "product terms," which are multiple logical signals ANDed together. The product terms are then ORed together. The Boolean equation in Figure 1.8 has four product terms.

In a PAL, unlike a PLA, the OR plane is fixed, limiting the number of terms that can be ORed together. This still allows a large number of Boolean equations to be implemented. The reason for this can be demonstrated by DeMorgan's Law, which states that a | b = !(!a & !b) or A OR B is equivalent to NOT(NOT A AND NOT B).

```
xyz =   a1 &  b1 &  c2
    | !a1 &  b1 & !c2
    |  a1 & !b1
    |  a1       & !c2
```

Figure 1.8   Boolean equation with four product terms

Figure 1.7   PAL architecture

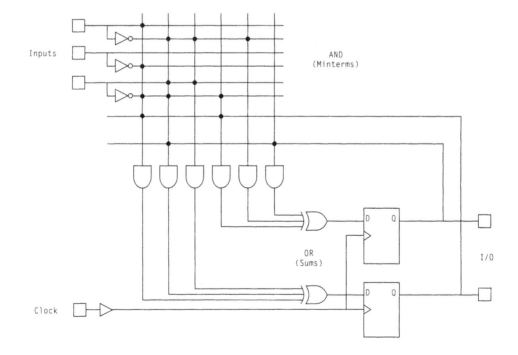

That means if you use inverters on the inputs and outputs, you can create all the logic you need with either a wide AND plane or a wide OR plane, but you don't need both.

Including inverters reduced the need for the large OR plane, which in turn allowed the extra silicon area on the chip to be used for other basic logic devices, such as multiplexers, exclusive ORs, and latches. Most importantly, clocked elements, typically flip-flops, could be included in PALs. These devices were now able to implement a large number of logic functions, including clocked sequential logic needed for state machines. This was an important development that allowed PALs to replace much of the standard logic in many designs. PALs are also extremely fast. With PALs, high-speed controllers could be designed in programmable logic.

Notice the architecture of a PAL, shown in Figure 1.7. The AND plane is shown in the upper-left corner as a switch matrix. The dots show where connections have been programmed. The fixed-size ORs are represented as OR gates. A clock input is used to clock the flip-flops. The outputs of the flip-flops can be driven off the chip, or they can be fed back to the AND plane in order to create a state machine.

The inclusion of extra logic devices, particularly flip-flops, greatly increased the complexity and potential uses of PALs, creating a need for new methods of programming that were flexible and readable. Thus the first hardware description languages (HDLs) were born. These simple HDLs included ABEL, CUPL, and PALASM, the precursors of Verilog and VHDL, much more complex languages that are in use today for CPLD, FPGA, and ASIC design.

A simple ABEL program for a PAL is shown in Listing 1.1. Don't worry about trying to understand the details — it's for illustration purposes only. Notice that the programming language allows the use of simulation test vectors in the code. The simulation vectors are at the end of the program. This simulation capability brought better reliability and verification of programmable devices, something that was critical when CPLDs and FPGAs were developed.

Listing 1.1   A simple ABEL program

```
MODULE DECODE;

FLAG '-R3','-T1','-V','-F0','-G','-Q2';

TITLE'
  CHIP        : Decode PAL - Version A
  DATE        : July 17, 1991
```

Listing 1.1   A simple ABEL program (Continued)

```
DESIGNER    : Bob Zeidman'

" PAL to decode addresses.

decode DEVICE 'P20R6';

"CONSTANTS:
  h = 1;
  l = 0;
  c = .C.;
  x = .X.;
  z = .Z.;

"INPUTS:
  clk       PIN  1;    "System clock
  !res      PIN  2;    "System reset
  !req      PIN  3;    "Instruction/Data Request from processor
  !emacc    PIN  4;    "Emulator access
  opt0      PIN  5;    "Opt bit from processor
  opt1      PIN  6;    "Opt bit from processor
  opt2      PIN  7;    "Opt bit from processor
  a19       PIN  8;    "Address bit from processor
  a20       PIN  9;    "Address bit from processor
  a21       PIN 10;    "Address bit from processor
  a22       PIN 11;    "Address bit from processor
  !oe       PIN 13;    "Output enable
  a23       PIN 14;    "Address bit from processor
  a31       PIN 23;    "Address bit from processor

"OUTPUTS:
  !sram     PIN 15;    "SRAM select
  !dram     PIN 16;    "DRAM select
  !parallel PIN 17;    "Parallel port select
  !leds     PIN 18;    "LEDs select
  !switch   PIN 19;    "Switches select
```

Listing 1.1   A simple ABEL program (Continued)

```
!serial    PIN 20;      "Serial port select
!config    PIN 21;      "Configuration register select
!eprom     PIN 22;      "EPROM select


"MEMORY MAP
addr      = [a31, a23, a22, a21, a20, a19];

EPROM     = [ 0,   0,   0,   0,   0,   x ];
SRAM      = [ 0,   0,   0,   0,   1,   0 ];
DRAM_LO   = [ 0,   0,   0,   0,   1,   1 ];
DRAM_HI   = [ 0,   1,   0,   0,   1,   0 ];
PARALLEL  = [ 0,   1,   0,   1,   0,   0 ];
SERIAL    = [ 0,   1,   0,   1,   0,   1 ];
SWITCHES  = [ 0,   1,   0,   1,   1,   0 ];
LEDS      = [ 0,   1,   0,   1,   1,   1 ];
CONFIG    = [ 0,   1,   1,   0,   0,   0 ];

EQUATIONS

  eprom     = req & !emacc & !opt2 & !res & (addr == EPROM);

  sram      = req & !emacc & !opt2 & !res & (addr == SRAM);

  dram     := req & !emacc & !opt2 & !res & (addr >= DRAM_LO) &
              (addr <= DRAM_HI);

  parallel := req & !emacc & !opt2 & !res & (addr == PARALLEL);

  serial   := req & !emacc & !opt2 & !res & (addr == SERIAL);

  switch   := req & !emacc & !opt2 & !res & !switch &
              (addr == SWITCHES);

  leds     := req & !emacc & !opt2 & !res & !leds & (addr == LEDS);
```

Listing 1.1   A simple ABEL program (Continued)

```
config   := req & !emacc & !opt2 & !res & !config &
            (addr == CONFIG);

TEST_VECTORS(
    [ clk, !res, !oe, !req, !emacc, opt2, opt1, opt0 ]
 -> [eprom,!sram,!dram,!parallel,!serial,!switch,!leds,!config]);
    [ c, 0, 0, x, x, x, x, x ] -> [ 1, 1, 1, 1, 1, 1, 1, 1 ];
    [ c, 1, 0, 1, x, x, x, x ] -> [ 1, 1, 1, 1, 1, 1, 1, 1 ];
    [ c, 1, 0, x, 0, x, x, x ] -> [ 1, 1, 1, 1, 1, 1, 1, 1 ];
    [ c, 1, 0, x, x, 1, x, x ] -> [ 1, 1, 1, 1, 1, 1, 1, 1 ];

TEST_VECTORS(
    [!res,!oe,!req,!emacc,opt2,opt1,opt0,a31,a23,a22,a21,a20,a19]
 -> [ !eprom, !sram ] );
"5"  [ 0, 0, x, x, x, x, x, x, x, x, x, x, x ] -> [ 1, 1 ];
    [ 1, 0, 1, x, x, x, x, x, x, x, x, x, x ] -> [ 1, 1 ];
    [ 1, 0, 0, 1, 0, x, x, 0, 0, 0, 0, 0, 0 ] -> [ 0, 1 ];
    [ 1, 0, 0, 1, 0, x, x, 0, 0, 0, 0, 0, 1 ] -> [ 0, 1 ];
    [ 1, 0, 0, 1, 0, x, x, 0, 0, 0, 0, 1, 0 ] -> [ 1, 0 ];
"10" [ 1, 0, 0, 1, 0, x, x, 0, 0, 0, 0, 1, 1 ] -> [ 1, 1 ];

END;
```

Listing 1.2 shows the compiled output from this code, consisting of a map of connections within the device to program in order to obtain the correct functionality.

Listing 1.2   The compiled output.

```
ABEL(tm) 3.00a FutureNet Div, Data I/O Corp.  JEDEC file for: P20R6
Created on: 29-Nov-:1 06:52 PM


  CHIP       : Decode PAL - Version A
  DATE       : July 17, 1991
  DESIGNER   : Bob Zeidman*
QP24* QF2560* QV10*
L0000
```

Listing 1.2   The compiled output. (Continued)

```
1111111111111111111111111111111111111111
0110101101111111111111011111111011101110110
0000000000000000000000000000000000000000
0000000000000000000000000000000000000000
0000000000000000000000000000000000000000
0000000000000000000000000000000000000000
0000000000000000000000000000000000000000
0000000000000000000000000000000000000000
0110101101011111111110111101111011101101101
0000000000000000000000000000000000000000
0000000000000000000000000000000000000000
0000000000000000000000000000000000000000
0000000000000000000000000000000000000000
0000000000000000000000000000000000000000
0000000000000000000000000000000000000000
0000000000000000000000000000000000000000
0000000000000000000000000000000000000000
0110101101111111111110110111011101101111001
0000000000000000000000000000000000000000
0000000000000000000000000000000000000000
0000000000000000000000000000000000000000
0000000000000000000000000000000000000000
0000000000000000000000000000000000000000
0000000000000000000000000000000000000000
0000000000000000000000000000000000000000
0110101101111111110110111011011101111001
0000000000000000000000000000000000000000
0000000000000000000000000000000000000000
0000000000000000000000000000000000000000
0000000000000000000000000000000000000000
0000000000000000000000000000000000000000
0000000000000000000000000000000000000000
0000000000000000000000000000000000000000
0110101101111111111110010111011101111001
0000000000000000000000000000000000000000
0000000000000000000000000000000000000000
```

Listing 1.2 **The compiled output. (Continued)**

```
0000000000000000000000000000000000000000
0000000000000000000000000000000000000000
0000000000000000000000000000000000000000
0000000000000000000000000000000000000000
0000000000000000000000000000000000000000
0110101101111111111110111011011101111001
0000000000000000000000000000000000000000
0000000000000000000000000000000000000000
0000000000000000000000000000000000000000
0000000000000000000000000000000000000000
0000000000000000000000000000000000000000
0000000000000000000000000000000000000000
0000000000000000000000000000000000000000
0110101101111111111110111011111110111001
0110101101111111111110111111011110111001
0110101101111111111110110110111111111110
0110101101111111111101111111111101111110
0110101101111111111101111111111111110110
0000000000000000000000000000000000000000
0000000000000000000000000000000000000000
0000000000000000000000000000000000000000
1111111111111111111111111111111111111111
0110101101111111111110111011011110111010
0000000000000000000000000000000000000000
0000000000000000000000000000000000000000
0000000000000000000000000000000000000000
0000000000000000000000000000000000000000
0000000000000000000000000000000000000000
0000000000000000000000000000000000000000*
V0001 C0XXXXXXXXXN0XHHHHHHHHXN*
V0002 C11XXXXXXXXN0XHHHHHHHHXN*
V0003 C1X0XXXXXXXN0XHHHHHHHHXN*
V0004 C1XXXX1XXXXN0XHHHHHHHHXN*
V0005 X0XXXXXXXXXN0XHNNNNNNNHXN*
V0006 X11XXXXXXXXN0XHNNNNNNNHXN*
```

Listing 1.2   The compiled output. (Continued)

```
V0007 X101XX00000N00HNNNNNNLON*
V0008 X101XX01000N00HNNNNNNLON*
V0009 X101XX00100N00LNNNNNNHON*
V0010 X101XX01100N00HNNNNNNHON*
C3B9E*
7519
```

1.4 The Masked Gate Array ASIC

An application specific integrated circuit, or ASIC, is not a programmable device, but it is important precursor to the developments leading up to CPLDs and FPGAs. An ASIC is a chip that an engineer can design with no particular knowledge of semiconductor physics or semiconductor processes. The ASIC vendor has created a library of cells and functions that the designer can use without needing to know precisely how these functions are implemented in silicon. The ASIC vendor also typically supports software tools that automate such processes as circuit synthesis and circuit layout. The ASIC vendor may even supply application engineers to assist the ASIC design engineer with the task. The vendor then lays out the chip, creates the masks, and manufactures the ASICs.

ASICs can be implemented using one of two internal architectures — gate array or standard cell. The differences between the two architectures are beyond the scope of this book. The standard cell architecture is not as relevant to CPLDs and FPGAs as the gate array architecture, which I describe briefly.

The gate array ASIC consists of rows and columns of regular transistor structures, as shown in Figure 1.9. Around the sides of the chip die are I/O cells containing input and output buffers along with some limited number of transistor. These I/O cells also contain the large bonding pads, shown in the figure, which are simply metal pads that are connected or "bonded" to the external pins of the chip using very small bonding wires.

Within the core array are basic cells, or gates, each consisting of some small number of transistors that are not connected. In fact, none of the transistors on the gate array are initially connected at all. The reason for this is that the connection is determined completely by the design that you implement. Once given a design, the layout software figures out which transistors to connect by placing metal connections on top of the die as shown. First, the low level functions are connected together. For example, six transistors could be connected to create a D flip-flop. These six transistors would be located physically very close to each

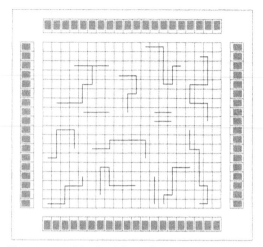

Figure 1.9   Masked Gate Array architecture

other. After the low level functions have been routed, they would in turn be connected together. The software would continue this process until the entire design is complete.

The ASIC vendor manufactures many unrouted die that contain the arrays of gates and that it can use for any gate array customer. An integrated circuit consists of many layers of materials, including semiconductor material (e.g., silicon), insulators (e.g., oxides), and conductors (e.g., metal). An unrouted die is processed with all of the layers except for the final metal layers that connect the gates together. Once the design is complete, the vendor simply needs to add the last metal layers to the die to create your chip, using photo masks for each metal layer. For this reason, it is sometimes referred to as a "masked gate array" to differentiate it from a field programmable gate array.

The advantage of a gate array is that the internal circuitry is very fast; the circuit is dense, allowing lots of functionality on a die; and the cost is low for high volume production. Gate arrays can reach clock frequencies of hundreds of megahertz with densities of millions of gates. The disadvantage is that it takes time for the ASIC vendor to manufacture and test the parts. Also, the customer incurs a large charge up front, called a non-recurring engineering (NRE) expense, which the ASIC vendor charges to begin the entire ASIC process. And if there's a mistake, it's a long, expensive process to fix it and manufacture new ASICs.

1.5 CPLDs and FPGAs

Ideally, hardware designers wanted something that gave them the advantages of an ASIC — circuit density and speed — but with the shorter turnaround time of a programmable device. The solution came in the form of two new devices — the complex pro-

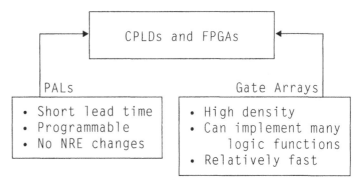

Figure 1.10 The evolution of CPLDs and FPGAs

grammable logic device (CPLD) and the field programmable gate array (FPGA). Figure 1.10 shows how CPLDs and FPGAs bridge the gap between PALs and gate arrays. All of the inherent advantages of PALs, shown on the left of the diagram, and all of the inherent advantages of gate array ASICS, shown on the right of the diagram, were combined. CPLDs are as fast as PALs but more complex. FPGAs approach the complexity of gate arrays but are still programmable. CPLD architectures and technologies are the same as those for PALs. FPGA architecture is similar to those of gate array ASICs.

1.6 Summary

Several programmable and semi-custom technologies preceded the development of CPLDs and FPGAs. This chapter started by reviewing the architecture, properties, uses, and tradeoffs of the various programmable devices (PROMS, PLAS, and PALs) that were in use before CPLDs and FPGAs. Later the chapter described ASICs and examined the contribution of a specific type of ASIC architecture called a gate array. The architecture, properties, uses, and tradeoffs of the gate array were discussed. Finally, CPLDs and FPGAs were introduced, briefly, as programmable chip solutions that filled the gap between programmable devices and gat array ASICs.

Exercises

1. What does the term ASIC stand for?
    (a) Application standard integrated chip
    (b) Applied system integrated circuit
    (c) Application specific integrated circuit

2. Match each programmable device with its description.

    (a) PROM   (A) A memory device that can be programmed once and read many times.

    (b) PLA   (B) A logic device that can be used to design large functions like an ASIC, except that it can be programmed quickly and inexpensively.

    (c) PAL   (C) A logic device that is made up of many PAL devices.

    (d) CPLD   (D) A logic device with a large AND plane and a large OR plane for implementing different combinations of Boolean logic.

    (e) FPGA   (E) A logic device with a large AND plane and a small, fixed number of OR gates for implementing Boolean logic and state machines.

3. Choose the correct device for each statement — PALs or ASICs.
    (a) _____ have a short lead time.
    (b) _____ are high-density devices.
    (c) _____ can implement very complex functions.
    (d) _____ do not have NRE charges.
    (e) _____ are programmable.

In this chapter...

- *CPLD Architectures*
- *Function Blocks*
- *I/O Blocks*
- *CPLD Technology and Programmable Elements*
- *CPLD Selection Criteria*
- *Example CPLD Families*

Chapter 2

Complex Programmable Logic Devices (CPLDs)

Complex Programmable Logic Devices are exactly what they claim to be: logic devices that are complex and programmable. There are two main engineering features to understand about CPLDs that separate them from their cousins, FPGAs. One feature is the internal architecture of the device and how this architecture implements various logic functions. The second feature is the semiconductor technology that allows the devices to be programmed and allows various structures in the device to be connected.

Objectives

This chapter focuses on the architecture and technologies of CPLDs. This chapter should help you:

- Understand the internal architecture of CPLDs
- Gain knowledge of the technologies used for programming and connecting internal blocks of CPLDs
- Learn the advantages and tradeoffs of different architectures and technologies

2.1 CPLD Architectures

Essentially, CPLDs are designed to appear just like a large number of PALs in a single chip, connected to each other through a crosspoint switch. This architecture made them familiar to their target market — PC board designers who were already designing PALs in their boards. Many CPLDs were used to simply combine multiple PALs in order to save real estate on a PC board. CPLDs use the same development tools and programmers as PALs, and are based on the same technologies as PALs, but they can handle much more complex logic and more of it.

The diagram in Figure 2.1 shows the internal architecture of a typical CPLD. Although each manufacturer has a different variation, in general they are all similar in that they consist of function blocks, input/output blocks, and an interconnect matrix.

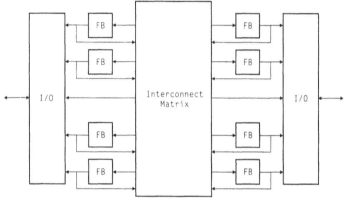

Figure 2.1   CPLD Architecture (courtesy of Altera Corporation)

2.2 Function Blocks

A typical function block is shown in Figure 2.3. Notice the similarity to the PAL architecture with its wide AND plane and fixed number of OR gates. The AND plane is shown by the crossing wires on the left. The AND plane can accept inputs from the I/O blocks, other function blocks, or feedback from the same function block. Programming elements at each

```
xyz =   a1 &  b1 &  c2
    |  !a1 &  b1 & !c2
    |   a1 & !b1
    |   a1       & !c2
```

Figure 2.2   Boolean equation with four product terms

intersection in the AND plane allow perpendicular traces to be connected or left open, creating "product terms," which are multiple signals ANDed together, just like in a PAL. The product terms are then ORed together and sent straight out of the block, or through a clocked flip-flop. The Boolean equation in Figure 2.2 has four product terms.

There are also multiplexers in the diagram, shown as boxes labeled M1, M2, and M3. Each mux has an FET transistor beneath it, representing a programmable element attached to the select line. In other words, the mux can be programmed to output one of the inputs. M1 is the "Clear Select" because it selects the signal that is used to clear the flip-flop. The M2 mux is labeled "Clock/Enable Select" because its two outputs are programmed to control the clock and clock enable input to the flip-flop. The M3 mux is labeled "Register Bypass" because it is programmed to determine whether the output of the functional block is a registered signal (i.e., is the output of a flip-flop) or a combinatorial signal (i.e., is the output of combinatorial logic).

Many CPLDs include additional, specialized logic. This particular block includes an exclusive OR, which can be effectively bypassed by programming one input to always be a 0. An XOR can be a nice gate to have because it is otherwise difficult to implement this function in a PAL. Exclusive ORs are used to easily generate parity in a bus for simple error detection.

Though not explicitly shown in Figure 2.3, each functional block would have many OR gates, logic gates, muxes, and flip-flops. Usually, the function blocks are designed to be similar to existing PAL architectures, such as the 22V10, so that the designer can use familiar tools to design them. They may even be able to fit older PAL designs into the CPLD without changing the design.

Figure 2.3   CPLD function block (courtesy of Altera Corporation)

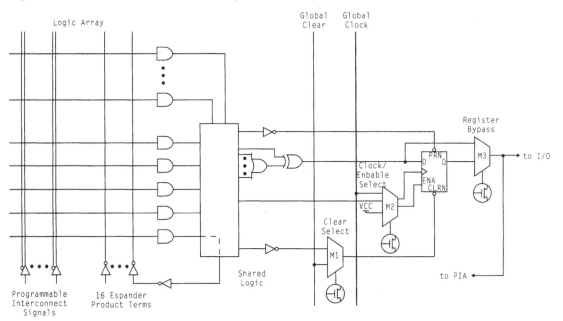

2.3 I/O Blocks

Figure 2.4 shows a typical I/O block of a CPLD. The I/O block is used to drive signals to the pins of the CPLD device at the appropriate voltage levels (e.g., TTL, CMOS, ECL, PECL, or LVDS). The I/O block typically allows each I/O pin to be individually configured for input, output, or bi-directional operation. The I/O pins have a tri-state output buffer that can be controlled by global output enable signals or directly connected to ground or VCC. Each output pin can also be configured to be open drain. In addition, outputs can often be programmed to drive different voltage levels, enabling the CPLD to be interfaced to many different devices.

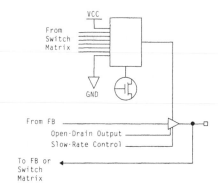

Figure 2.4   CPLD input/output block (courtesy of Altera Corporation)

One particularly useful feature in high speed CPLDs is the ability to control the rise and fall rates of the output drivers by using a slew rate control. Designers can configure the output buffers for fast rise and fall times or for slow transition times. An advantage of the fast speed of these devices is less delay through the logic. A disadvantage of faster transition is times that they can cause overshoot and undershoot, which can potentially damage the device that the CPLD is driving. Also, fast transitions introduce noise, which can create problems. By programming the slew rate of the output buffer to a relatively slow transition, you can preserve the small logic delays of the device while avoiding undershoot, overshoot, and noise problems.

The input signal from the I/O block goes into the switch matrix in order to be routed to the appropriate functional block. In some architectures, particular inputs have direct paths to particular functional blocks in order to lower the delay on the input, reducing the signal setup time. In most architectures, specific pins of the device connect to specific I/O blocks that can drive global signals like reset and clock. This means that only certain pins of the device can be used to drive these global signals. This is particularly important for clock signals, as described in the next section.

2.4 Clock Drivers

As Section 5.3 (in Chapter 5) explains, synchronous design is the only accepted design methodology that will ensure that a CPLD-based design is reliable over its lifetime. In order to design synchronous CPLDs, the clock signal must arrive at each flip-flop in the design at about the same time and with very little delay from the input pin. In order to accomplish this, special I/O blocks have clock drivers that use very fast input buffers and which drive the input clock signal onto an internal clock tree. The clock tree is so named because it resembles a tree, with each branch driving the clock input of a fixed number of flip-flops. The clock driver is designed to drive the entire tree very quickly. The trees are designed to minimize the skew between clock signals arriving at different flip-flops throughout the device. Each branch of the tree is of approximately equal length, or if not, internal buffers are used to balance the skew along the different branches. It is important that clock signals are only driven through the clock input pins that connect to these special drivers.

In large devices, there may be several clock input pins connected to different clock drivers. This feature helps in designs that use multiple clocks. You need to have at least as many clock drivers in the CPLD as you need clocks in your design. Also, the different clocks must be considered to be asynchronous with respect to each other, because the CPLD vendor does not typically guarantee skew between multiple clocks. Signals clocked by one clock will need to be synchronized with the other clock before use by any logic clocked by the second clock. For more information on synchronous design and synchronizing asynchronous signals, see Section 5.3.

2.5 Interconnect

The CPLD interconnect is a very large programmable switch matrix that allows signals from all parts of the device to go to all other parts of the device. Figure 2.5 shows the architecture of the switch matrix. The switch matrix takes the outputs of the functional blocks and is programmed to send those outputs to functional blocks. This way, the designer can route any output signal to any destination.

Computing Parity Without Exclusive OR

The Boolean expression for generating even parity for a bus is shown in the following equation:

```
parity = a0 ^ a1 ^ a2 ^ a3 ^ a4 ^ a5 ^ a6 ^ a7
```

If we implement this equation using AND and OR logic, the result is

```
parity =    a0 & !a1 & !a2 & !a3 & !a4 & !a5 & !a6 & !a7
        | !a0 &  a1 & !a2 & !a3 & !a4 & !a5 & !a6 & !a7
        |  a0 &  a1 &  a2 & !a3 & !a4 & !a5 & !a6 & !a7
        | !a0 & !a1 &  a2 & !a3 & !a4 & !a5 & !a6 & !a7
        |  a0 & !a1 &  a2 &  a3 & !a4 & !a5 & !a6 & !a7
        | !a0 &  a1 &  a2 &  a3 & !a4 & !a5 & !a6 & !a7
        |  a0 &  a1 & !a2 &  a3 & !a4 & !a5 & !a6 & !a7
        | !a0 & !a1 & !a2 &  a3 & !a4 & !a5 & !a6 & !a7
        |  a0 & !a1 & !a2 &  a3 &  a4 & !a5 & !a6 & !a7
        | !a0 &  a1 & !a2 &  a3 &  a4 & !a5 & !a6 & !a7
        |  a0 &  a1 &  a2 &  a3 &  a4 & !a5 & !a6 & !a7
        | !a0 & !a1 &  a2 &  a3 &  a4 & !a5 & !a6 & !a7
        |  a0 & !a1 &  a2 & !a3 &  a4 & !a5 & !a6 & !a7
        | !a0 &  a1 &  a2 & !a3 &  a4 & !a5 & !a6 & !a7
        |  a0 &  a1 & !a2 & !a3 &  a4 & !a5 & !a6 & !a7
        | !a0 & !a1 & !a2 & !a3 &  a4 & !a5 & !a6 & !a7
        |  a0 & !a1 & !a2 & !a3 &  a4 &  a5 & !a6 & !a7
        | !a0 &  a1 & !a2 & !a3 &  a4 &  a5 & !a6 & !a7
        |  a0 &  a1 &  a2 & !a3 &  a4 &  a5 & !a6 & !a7
        | !a0 & !a1 &  a2 & !a3 &  a4 &  a5 & !a6 & !a7
        |  a0 & !a1 &  a2 &  a3 &  a4 &  a5 & !a6 & !a7
        | !a0 &  a1 &  a2 &  a3 &  a4 &  a5 & !a6 & !a7
        |  a0 &  a1 & !a2 &  a3 &  a4 &  a5 & !a6 & !a7
        | !a0 & !a1 & !a2 &  a3 &  a4 &  a5 & !a6 & !a7
        |  a0 & !a1 & !a2 &  a3 & !a4 &  a5 & !a6 & !a7
        | !a0 &  a1 & !a2 &  a3 & !a4 &  a5 & !a6 & !a7
        |  a0 &  a1 &  a2 &  a3 & !a4 &  a5 & !a6 & !a7
        | !a0 & !a1 &  a2 &  a3 & !a4 &  a5 & !a6 & !a7
        |  a0 & !a1 &  a2 & !a3 & !a4 &  a5 & !a6 & !a7
        | !a0 &  a1 &  a2 & !a3 & !a4 &  a5 & !a6 & !a7
        |  a0 &  a1 & !a2 & !a3 & !a4 &  a5 & !a6 & !a7
        | !a0 & !a1 & !a2 & !a3 & !a4 &  a5 & !a6 & !a7
```

One advantage of the CPLD switch matrix routing scheme is that delays through the chip are deterministic. Designers can determine the delay for any signal by computing the delay through functional blocks, I/O blocks, and the switch matrix. All of these delays are fixed, and delays due to routing the signal along the metal traces are negligible. If the logic for a particular function is com-

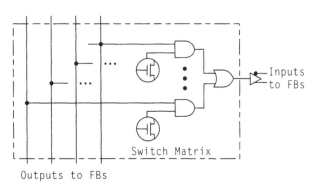

Figure 2.5   CPLD switch matrix (courtesy of Altera Corporation)

plex, it may require several functional blocks, and thus several passes through the switch matrix, to implement. Designers can bery easily calculate delays from input pins to output pins of a CPLD by using a few worst-case timing numbers supplied by the CPLD vendor. This contrasts greatly with FPGAs, which have very unpredictable and design-dependent timing due to their routing mechanism.

2.6 CPLD Technology and Programmable Elements

Different manufacturers use different technologies to implement the programmable elements of a CPLD. The common technologies are EPROM, EEPROM, and Flash EPROM. These technologies are versions of the technologies that were used for the simplest programmable devices, PROMs, which we discussed earlier. In functional blocks and I/O blocks, single bits are programmed to turn specific functions on and off, Figure 2.3 and Figure 2.4 show. In the switch matrix, single bits are programmed to control connections between signals using a multiplexer, as shown in Figure 2.5.

When PROM technology is used for these devices, they can be programmed only once. More commonly these days, manufacturers use EPROM, EEPROM, or Flash EPROM, allowing the devices to be erased and reprogrammed.

Erasable technology can also allow in-system programmability of the device. For CPLDs with this capability, a serial interface on the chip is used to send new programming data into the chip after it is soldered into a PC board and while the system is operating. Typically this serial interface is the industry-standard 4-pin Joint Test Action Group (JTAG) interface (IEEE Std. 1149.1-1990).

Computing Parity Without Exclusive OR (Continued)

```
|  a0 & !a1 & !a2 & !a3 & !a4 &  a5 &  a6 & !a7
| !a0 &  a1 & !a2 & !a3 & !a4 &  a5 &  a6 & !a7
|  a0 &  a1 &  a2 & !a3 & !a4 &  a5 &  a6 & !a7
| !a0 & !a1 &  a2 & !a3 & !a4 &  a5 &  a6 & !a7
|  a0 & !a1 &  a2 &  a3 & !a4 &  a5 &  a6 & !a7
| !a0 &  a1 &  a2 &  a3 & !a4 &  a5 &  a6 & !a7
|  a0 &  a1 & !a2 &  a3 & !a4 &  a5 &  a6 & !a7
| !a0 & !a1 & !a2 &  a3 & !a4 &  a5 &  a6 & !a7
|  a0 & !a1 & !a2 &  a3 &  a4 &  a5 &  a6 & !a7
| !a0 &  a1 & !a2 &  a3 &  a4 &  a5 &  a6 & !a7
|  a0 &  a1 &  a2 &  a3 &  a4 &  a5 &  a6 & !a7
| !a0 & !a1 &  a2 &  a3 &  a4 &  a5 &  a6 & !a7
|  a0 & !a1 &  a2 & !a3 &  a4 &  a5 &  a6 & !a7
| !a0 &  a1 &  a2 & !a3 &  a4 &  a5 &  a6 & !a7
|  a0 &  a1 & !a2 & !a3 &  a4 &  a5 &  a6 & !a7
| !a0 & !a1 & !a2 & !a3 &  a4 &  a5 &  a6 & !a7
|  a0 & !a1 & !a2 & !a3 &  a4 & !a5 &  a6 & !a7
| !a0 &  a1 & !a2 & !a3 &  a4 & !a5 &  a6 & !a7
|  a0 &  a1 &  a2 & !a3 &  a4 & !a5 &  a6 & !a7
| !a0 & !a1 &  a2 & !a3 &  a4 & !a5 &  a6 & !a7
|  a0 & !a1 &  a2 &  a3 &  a4 & !a5 &  a6 & !a7
| !a0 &  a1 &  a2 &  a3 &  a4 & !a5 &  a6 & !a7
|  a0 &  a1 & !a2 &  a3 &  a4 & !a5 &  a6 & !a7
| !a0 & !a1 & !a2 &  a3 &  a4 & !a5 &  a6 & !a7
|  a0 & !a1 & !a2 &  a3 & !a4 & !a5 &  a6 & !a7
| !a0 &  a1 & !a2 &  a3 & !a4 & !a5 &  a6 & !a7
|  a0 &  a1 &  a2 &  a3 & !a4 & !a5 &  a6 & !a7
| !a0 & !a1 &  a2 &  a3 & !a4 & !a5 &  a6 & !a7
|  a0 & !a1 &  a2 & !a3 & !a4 & !a5 &  a6 & !a7
| !a0 &  a1 &  a2 & !a3 & !a4 & !a5 &  a6 & !a7
|  a0 &  a1 & !a2 & !a3 & !a4 & !a5 &  a6 & !a7
| !a0 & !a1 & !a2 & !a3 & !a4 & !a5 &  a6 & !a7
|  a0 & !a1 & !a2 & !a3 & !a4 & !a5 &  a6 &  a7
| !a0 &  a1 & !a2 & !a3 & !a4 & !a5 &  a6 &  a7
|  a0 &  a1 &  a2 & !a3 & !a4 & !a5 &  a6 &  a7
| !a0 & !a1 &  a2 & !a3 & !a4 & !a5 &  a6 &  a7
|  a0 & !a1 &  a2 &  a3 & !a4 & !a5 &  a6 &  a7
```

2.7 Embedded Devices

A relatively recent addition to the architecture of many CPLD devices is embedded devices, which consists of large devices integrated into the CPLD. These devices can be connected to the rest of the CPLD via the switch matrix. The availability of embedded devices brings designers closer to the concept of a system on a programmable chip (SOPC). Engineers can now move the processors, memory, and other complex standard devices that would normally be on a circuit board along with a CPLD directly into the CPLD.

Table 2.1   JTAG signals

Signal	Description
TCK	Test Clock Input A clock signal used to shift test instructions, test data, and control inputs into the chip on the rising edge and to shift the output data from the chip on the falling edge.
TMS	Test Mode Select Serial input for controlling the internal JTAG state machine. The state of this bit on the rising edge of each clock determines which actions the chip is to take.
TDI	Test Data Input Serial input for instructions and program data. Data is captured on the rising edge of the clock.
TDO	Test Data Output Serial output for test instruction and program data from the chip. Valid data is driven out on the falling edge of the clock.
TRST	Test Reset Input (Extended JTAG only) An asynchronous active low reset that is used to initialize the JTAG controller.

The main advantages of embedded devices are cost reduction, reduced circuit board space, and often lower power consumption. A disadvantage is that it tends to tie your design into a specific CPLD offered by a single CPLD vendor because different vendors supply different embedded devices in their CPLDs, if they offer them at all.

The number and kinds of embedded devices that are being integrated into CPLDs are increasing annually. Currently, these devices include

- SRAM memories
- Flash memories

Computing Parity Without Exclusive OR (Continued)

```
|  !a0 &  a1 &  a2 &  a3 & !a4 & !a5 &  a6 &  a7
|   a0 &  a1 & !a2 &  a3 & !a4 & !a5 &  a6 &  a7
|  !a0 & !a1 & !a2 &  a3 & !a4 & !a5 &  a6 &  a7
|   a0 & !a1 & !a2 &  a3 &  a4 & !a5 &  a6 &  a7
|  !a0 &  a1 & !a2 &  a3 &  a4 & !a5 &  a6 &  a7
|   a0 &  a1 &  a2 &  a3 &  a4 & !a5 &  a6 &  a7
|  !a0 & !a1 &  a2 &  a3 &  a4 & !a5 &  a6 &  a7
|   a0 & !a1 &  a2 & !a3 &  a4 & !a5 &  a6 &  a7
|  !a0 &  a1 &  a2 & !a3 &  a4 & !a5 &  a6 &  a7
|   a0 &  a1 & !a2 & !a3 &  a4 & !a5 &  a6 &  a7
|  !a0 & !a1 & !a2 & !a3 &  a4 & !a5 &  a6 &  a7
|   a0 & !a1 & !a2 & !a3 &  a4 &  a5 &  a6 &  a7
|  !a0 &  a1 & !a2 & !a3 &  a4 &  a5 &  a6 &  a7
|   a0 &  a1 &  a2 & !a3 &  a4 &  a5 &  a6 &  a7
|  !a0 & !a1 &  a2 & !a3 &  a4 &  a5 &  a6 &  a7
|   a0 & !a1 &  a2 &  a3 &  a4 &  a5 &  a6 &  a7
|  !a0 &  a1 &  a2 &  a3 &  a4 &  a5 &  a6 &  a7
|   a0 &  a1 & !a2 &  a3 &  a4 &  a5 &  a6 &  a7
|  !a0 & !a1 & !a2 &  a3 &  a4 &  a5 &  a6 &  a7
|   a0 & !a1 & !a2 &  a3 & !a4 &  a5 &  a6 &  a7
|  !a0 &  a1 & !a2 &  a3 & !a4 &  a5 &  a6 &  a7
|   a0 &  a1 &  a2 &  a3 & !a4 &  a5 &  a6 &  a7
|  !a0 & !a1 &  a2 &  a3 & !a4 &  a5 &  a6 &  a7
|   a0 & !a1 &  a2 & !a3 & !a4 &  a5 &  a6 &  a7
|  !a0 &  a1 &  a2 & !a3 & !a4 &  a5 &  a6 &  a7
|   a0 &  a1 & !a2 & !a3 & !a4 &  a5 &  a6 &  a7
|  !a0 & !a1 & !a2 & !a3 & !a4 &  a5 &  a6 &  a7
|   a0 & !a1 & !a2 & !a3 & !a4 &  a5 & !a6 &  a7
|  !a0 &  a1 & !a2 & !a3 & !a4 &  a5 & !a6 &  a7
|   a0 &  a1 &  a2 & !a3 & !a4 &  a5 & !a6 &  a7
|  !a0 & !a1 &  a2 & !a3 & !a4 &  a5 & !a6 &  a7
|   a0 & !a1 &  a2 &  a3 & !a4 &  a5 & !a6 &  a7
|  !a0 &  a1 &  a2 &  a3 & !a4 &  a5 & !a6 &  a7
|   a0 &  a1 & !a2 &  a3 & !a4 &  a5 & !a6 &  a7
|  !a0 & !a1 & !a2 &  a3 & !a4 &  a5 & !a6 &  a7
|   a0 & !a1 &a2 &  a3 &  a4 &  a5 & !a6 &  a7
|  !a0 &  a1 & !a2 &  a3 &  a4 &  a5 & !a6 &  a7
```

Note
_____

JTAG interface

The JTAG interface, IEEE Standard 1149.1, is a simple serial interface specification created by the Joint Test Action Group of the Institute of Electrical and Electronic Engineers. This interface is typically used for adding boundary scan testability to a chip. Recently, though, programmers have begun using JTAG for programming CPLDs and FPGAs while the chip is in an active system. This capability is called in-system programming, or ISP.

A JTAG interface is defined as having four pins, as described in Table 2.1 (page 25). Extended JTAG includes a fifth reset pin. Instructions can be serially shifted into the chip on the TDI input. The TMS input controls the stepping through internal state machines to allow the programming of the device. Internal registers and the current state of the state machine can be shifted out via the TDO pin. The TRST pin is used to asynchronously initialize the internal state machine to prepare the chip for programming.
_____

- microcontrollers
- microprocessors
- Digital Signal Processors (DSPs)
- Phase Locked Loops (PLLs)
- network processors

2.8 Summary: CPLD Selection Criteria

The internal architecture and the semiconductor technology used to implement it's programmable elements strongly influence how well it "fits" a particular application. When designing a CPLD you should take the following architectural and technological issues into account:

- The programming technology — PROM, EPROM, EEPROM, or Flash EPROM. This will determine the equipment you will need to program the devices and whether they can be programmed only once or many times. The ability to reprogram during development will reduce your cost for parts, though that's not usually a significant part of the entire development cost.

- In-system programmability — This feature will allow engineers to update functionality in the field. This creates many options for upgrading existing customers, including network or Internet-based upgrades and fully automatic upgrades via software. Of course, developing the software to support an in-field upgrade for a system may require a lot of effort. Sending personnel out to upgrade hardware manually may or may not be cost effective for all applications. And the CPLDs in some systems simply cannot be disabled in

Computing Parity Without Exclusive OR (Continued)

```
|   a0 &  a1 &  a2 &  a3 &  a4 &  a5 & !a6 &  a7
|  !a0 & !a1 &  a2 &  a3 &  a4 &  a5 & !a6 &  a7
|   a0 & !a1 &  a2 & !a3 &  a4 &  a5 & !a6 &  a7
|  !a0 &  a1 &  a2 & !a3 &  a4 &  a5 & !a6 &  a7
|   a0 &  a1 & !a2 & !a3 &  a4 &  a5 & !a6 &  a7
|  !a0 & !a1 & !a2 & !a3 &  a4 &  a5 & !a6 &  a7
|   a0 & !a1 & !a2 &  a3 &  a4 & !a5 & !a6 &  a7
|  !a0 &  a1 & !a2 &  a3 &  a4 & !a5 & !a6 &  a7
|   a0 &  a1 &  a2 &  a3 &  a4 & !a5 & !a6 &  a7
|  !a0 & !a1 &  a2 & !a3 &  a4 & !a5 & !a6 &  a7
|   a0 & !a1 &  a2 &  a3 &  a4 & !a5 & !a6 &  a7
|  !a0 &  a1 &  a2 &  a3 &  a4 & !a5 & !a6 &  a7
|   a0 &  a1 & !a2 &  a3 &  a4 & !a5 & !a6 &  a7
|  !a0 & !a1 & !a2 &  a3 &  a4 & !a5 & !a6 &  a7
|   a0 & !a1 & !a2 &  a3 & !a4 & !a5 & !a6 &  a7
|  !a0 &  a1 & !a2 &  a3 & !a4 & !a5 & !a6 &  a7
|   a0 &  a1 &  a2 &  a3 & !a4 & !a5 & !a6 &  a7
|  !a0 & !a1 &  a2 &  a3 & !a4 & !a5 & !a6 &  a7
|   a0 & !a1 &  a2 & !a3 & !a4 & !a5 & !a6 &  a7
|  !a0 &  a1 &  a2 & !a3 & !a4 & !a5 & !a6 &  a7
|   a0 &  a1 & !a2 & !a3 & !a4 & !a5 & !a6 &  a7
|  !a0 & !a1 & !a2 & !a3 & !a4 & !a5 & !a6 &  a7)
```

As you can see, this requires a large number of AND gates and OR gates. In a typical PAL or CPLD, there are many AND gates that can be used, through DeMorgan's Law, as OR gates, but we do not have the resources for a large number of both AND and OR gates. Thus, including an XOR in the functional block makes implementation of parity practical.

Note that the flip-flop in this functional block has an asynchronous preset and a synchronous clear. The preset is controlled by the logic in the functional block, whereas the reset can be controlled by the logic of the functional block or by a global clear signal used to initialize each flip-flop in the entire device. The flip-flop clock can also be generated from the functional block logic as well as from a global clock line, as is the case for the clock enable input for the flip-flop. Note that not every CPLD from every manufacturer has all of these capabilities for the flip-flops. Also note that when I discuss synchronous design, in Section 5.3, you will see that, for reliability reasons, that clocks and asynchronous inputs should only be controlled by the global signal lines and not by any internal logic, even though the CPLD may give that ability.

the field, so in-system programmability may not be an option. Consider all of these factors before deciding whether this feature is useful for the design.

- The function block capability — Although most CPLDs have similar function blocks, there are differences, for example, in the number of flip-flops and the number of inputs to each block. Try to find a function block architecture that fits your design. If the design is dominated by combinatorial logic, you will prefer function blocks with large numbers of inputs. If the design performs a lot of parity checking, you will prefer function blocks with built-in XOR gates. If the design has many pipelined stages, you will prefer function blocks with several flip-flops.

- The number of function blocks in the device — This will determine how much logic the device can hold and how easily the design will fit into it.

- The kind of flip-flop controls available (e.g., clock enable, reset, preset, polarity control) and the number of global controls — CPLDs typically have global resets that simplify the design for initializing registers and state machines. Clock enables can often be useful in state machine design if you can take advantage of them.

- Embedded devices — Does the design interface with devices like a microcontroller or a PLL? Many CPLDs now incorporate specialized functions like these, which will make your job much easier and allow you to integrate more devices into a single CPLD.

- The number and type of I/O pins — Obviously, the CPLD will need to support the number of I/O pins in your design. Also, determine how many of these are general purpose I/O and how many are reserved for special functions like clock input, master reset, etc.

- The number of clock input pins — Clock signals can be driven only into particular pins. If the design has several clock domains (i.e., sections driven by separate clocks), you will need a CPLD that has that many clock input pins.

You must take into account other issues for all programmable chips that you intend to use in the design. For a list of these general issues, refer to Section 4.2 about the chip specification.

Exercises

1. What does the term CPLD mean?
   (a) Complex programmable logic device
   (b) Combinatorial programmable logic device
   (c) Combinatorial programmable local device

2. Select all of the parts of a typical CPLD.
   (a) I/O block
   (b) ALU block
   (c) Decode logic
   (d) Function block
   (e) Interconnect matrix

3. Which technology is not used for CPLD programmable elements?
   (a) Flash EPROM
   (b) EEPROM
   (c) EPROM
   (d) DRAM

4. Which is not a characteristic of clock drivers?
   (a) High current output
   (b) Drives many flip-flops
   (c) Low power
   (d) Are the only acceptable means of driving clock signals

5. The layout of traces that connects a clock driver to the flip-flops in a CPLD is called
   (a) A clock tree
   (b) A long line
   (c) A short line
   (d) Synchronous design

6. One advantage of the CPLD switch matrix routing scheme is that delays through the chip are
    (a) Less than a nanosecond
    (b) Deterministic
    (c) Slow
    (d) Adjustable

7. Embedded devices are (select one)
    (a) Devices that are used for programming CPLDs
    (b) Devices that are embedded inside a CPLD
    (c) CPLDs that can be embedded into an ASIC
    (d) Any device that is created from one or more CPLDs

Chapter 3

Field Programmable Gate Arrays (FPGAs)

Field Programmable Gate Arrays are given this name because they are structured very much like a gate array ASIC. Like an ASIC, the FPGA consists of a regular array of logic, an architecture that lends itself to very complex designs.

Objectives

This chapter describes the architecture and technologies of FPGAs. This chapter should help you:

- Understand the internal architecture of FPGAs
- Gain knowledge of the technologies used for programming and connecting internal blocks of FPGAs
- Learn the advantages and trade-offs of different architectures and technologies
- Learn the differences between CPLDs and FPGAs

3.1 FPGA Architectures

Each FPGA vendor has its own FPGA architecture, but in general terms they are all a variation of that shown in Figure 3.1. The architecture consists of configurable logic blocks, configurable I/O blocks, and programmable interconnect to route signals between the logic blocks and I/O blocks. Also, there is clock circuitry for driving the clock signals to each flip-flop in each logic block. Additional logic resources such as ALUs, memory, and decoders may also be available. The two most common types of programmable elements for an FPGA are static RAM and antifuses. Antifuse technology is a cousin to the programmable fuses in EPROMs. You will learn about antifuses, along with these other aspects of FPGAs, in the following sections.

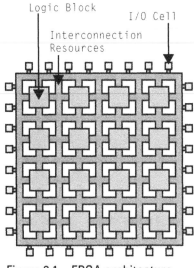

Figure 3.1   FPGA architecture

The important thing to note about the FPGA architecture is its regular, ASIC-like structure. This regular structure makes FPGAs useful for all kinds of logic designs.

3.2 Configurable Logic Blocks

Configurable logic blocks (CLBs) contain the programmable logic for the FPGA. The diagram in Figure 3.2 shows a typical CLB, containing RAM for creating arbitrary combinatorial logic functions. It also contains flip-flops for clocked storage elements and multiplexers in order to route the logic within the block and to route the logic to and from external resources. These muxes also allow polarity selection, reset input, and clear input selection.

On the left of the CLB are two 4-input memories, also known as 4-input lookup tables or 4-LUTs. As discussed in an earlier chapter, 4-input memories can produce any possible 4-input Boolean equation. Feeding the output of the two 4-LUTs into a 3-LUT, produces a wide variety of outputs (for up to nine inputs).

Four signals labeled C1 through C4 enter at the top of the CLB. These are inputs from other CLBs or I/O blocks on the chip, allowing outputs from other CLBs to be input to this particular CLB. These interconnect inputs allow designers to partition large logic functions among several CLBs. They also are the basis for connecting CLBs in order to create a large, functioning design.

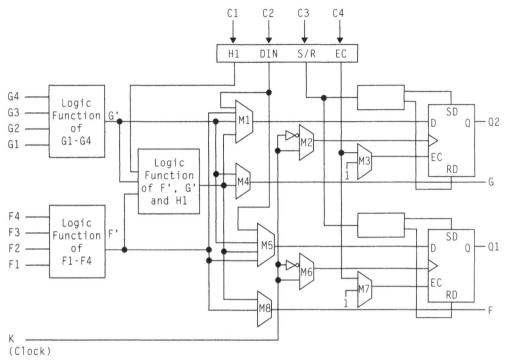

Figure 3.2   FPGA configurable logic block (CLB) (courtesy of Xilinx Inc.)

The muxes throughout the CLB are programmed statically. In other words, when the FPGA is programmed, the select lines are set high or low and remain in that state. Some muxes allow signal paths through the chip to be programmed. For example, mux M1 is programmed so that the top right flip-flop data is either input C2, or the output of one of the two 4-LUTs or the output of the 3-LUT.

Some muxes are programmed to affect the operation of the CLB flip-flops. Mux M2 is programmed to allow the top flip-flop to transition on the rising or falling edge of the clock signal. Mux M3 is programmed to always enable the top flip-flop, or to enable only when input signal C4 is asserted to enable it.

Note that the clock input to the flip-flops must come only from the global clock signal. Earlier architectures allowed flip-flops to be clocked by the outputs of the combinatorial logic. This allowed asynchronous designs that created lots of problems, as I discuss later in Section 6.3, and FPGA vendors eventually took that capability out of their architectures, greatly reducing their headaches and greatly increasing the reliability of their customers' designs.

Note that the logic outputs do not need to go through the flip-flops. Designers can use a CLB to create simple combinatorial logic. Because of this, multiple CLBs can, and often are, connected together to implement complex Boolean logic. This advantage of FPGAs over CPLDs means that designers can implement very complex logic by stringing together several CLBs. Unfortunately, routing delay in an FPGA is a significant amount of the overall delay. So this advantage also results in an overall decrease in the speed of the design.

Fine-grained vs. large-grained CLBs

In theory, there are two types of CLBs, depending on the amount and type of logic that is contained within them. These two types are called "large grain" and "fine grain."

In a large grain FPGA, the CLB contains larger functionality logic. For example, it can contain two or more flip-flops. A design that does not need many flip-flops will leave many of these flip-flops unused, poorly utilizing the logic resources in the CLBs and in the chip. A design that requires lots of combinatorial logic will be required to use up the LUTs in the CLBs while leaving the flip-flops untouched.

Fine grain FPGAs resemble ASIC gate arrays in that the CLBs contain only small, very basic elements such as NAND gates, NOR gates, etc. The philosophy is that small elements can be connected to make larger functions without wasting too much logic. If a flip-flop is needed, one can be constructed by connecting NAND gates. If it's not needed, then the NAND gates can be used for other features. In theory, this apparent efficiency seemed to be an advantage. Also, because they more closely resembled ASICs, it seemed that any eventual conversion of the FPGA to ASIC would be easier.

However, one key fact renders the fine grain architecture less useful and less efficient. It turns out that routing resources are the bottleneck in any FPGA design in terms of utilization and speed. In other words, it is often difficult to connect CLBs together using the limited routing resources on the chip. Also, in an FPGA, unlike an ASIC, the majority of the delay comes from routing, not logic. Fine grain architectures require many more routing resources, which take up space and insert a large amount of delay, which can more than compensate for their better utilization. This is why all FPGA vendors currently use large grain architectures for their CLBs.

In the early days of the industry several FPGA manufacturers produced fine grain architectures for their devices. Thinking like ASIC vendors, they missed the significance of the routing issues. All of these vendors have either fallen by the wayside or have abandoned their fine grain architectures for large grain ones.

3.3 Configurable I/O Blocks

A configurable I/O block, shown in Figure 3.3, is used to bring signals onto the chip and send them back off again. The output buffer, B1, has programmable controls to make the buffer three-state or open collector and to control the slew rate. These controls allow the FPGA to output to most standard TTL or CMOS devices. The slew rate control, as discussed in Chapter 2, is important in controlling noise, signal reflections, and overshoot and undershoot on today's very fast parts. Slowing signal rise and fall times, reduces the noise in a system and reduces overshoot, undershoot, and reflections.

The input buffer B2 can be programmed for different threshold voltages, typically TTL or CMOS level, in order to interface with TTL or CMOS devices. The combination of input and output buffers on each pin, and their programmability, means that each I/O block can be used for an input, an output, or a bi-directional signal.

The pull-up resistors in the I/O blocks are a nice feature. They take up little space in the FPGA and can be used to pull up three-state buses on a board. As I discuss Chapter 6, "Verification", floating buses increase the noise in a system, increase the power consumption, and have the potential to create metastability problems.

There are two small logic blocks in each I/O block, labeled L1 and L2 in the diagram. These blocks are there for two reasons. First, it always makes sense to

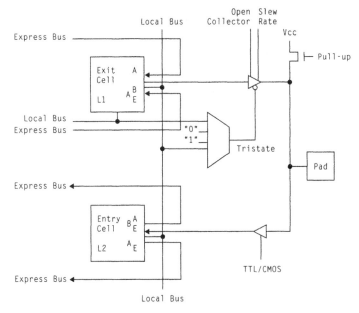

Figure 3.3   FPGA configurable I/O block (courtesy of Xilinx Inc.)

Pull-ups, Floating Buses, and Stubbornness

I would think it's obvious to anyone who understands CMOS technology that floating buses are bad. CMOS devices dissipate power unnecessarily when the inputs are floating, and floating signals are more prone to noise. A pull-up resistor is a very simple, small, low-power, inexpensive solution to the problem of floating buses. In my career, though, I have encountered, on two occasions, a religious fervor about not putting pull-ups on potentially floating buses. I still don't completely understand the reasons.

In one case, a career marketing manager at a large semiconductor company, who still prided himself on being a top-notch engineer, did a board design that I was asked to optimize, lay out, and debug. When I saw that he had omitted any pull-up resistors, I simply put them back in the schematic. When he saw this, he became angry. He told me that in all his years, he had never seen a problem, nor had he ever encountered a metastability problem. I replied that a reliability problem like metastability might only be seen once every year on a continually running board. It's not something that can be measured. This manager went so far as to inform the layout designer to tell me that she couldn't fit the pull-up resistor pack (nine pins on a small sliver of material) on the board. I could tell she felt ridiculous about this because she was telling me that she couldn't do something that any fresh-out-of-school layout designer could accomplish with the cheapest layout software package available.

In the other case, I was brought in to do a sanity check of a board design that was nearing completion. A small startup had a contract to design some specialized network boards for Cisco Systems. A consultant had been hired to design the board, and the project manager then hired me to review the design. In my review, one of the potential problems I found was, yes, no pull-up resistors on the buses. I mentioned this casually, and the board designer became irate for the same reasons as the manager I had met. There was no reason for it. They were too expensive (actually about $.01 per resistor), and they took up too much space (a pack of ten resistors takes a few square millimeters). Finally he said, "We met with those guys at Cisco and they said the same thing. They wanted those stupid, unnecessary resistors on the buses. I just won't waste my time doing it." Later, in private, I talked with the project manager. "You may not think there's a need for those resistors," I said, "and you may not trust my judgment. But if I were selling boards to Cisco and they said to spread peanut butter on the boards, I'd break out the Skippy®."

The point of these stories is that internal resistors on I/O pins of FPGAs make this problem go away. With internal resistors on the I/O pins, you can connect pull-ups to all of your buses, saving the tiny cost and area of a resistor pack, and no one will be the wiser.

stick logic wherever there is space for it. In the I/O block, there is space for it. Second, unlike an ASIC, the routing delay in an FPGA is much more significant than the logic delay. In an ASIC, signals are routed using metal layers, leading to RC delays that are insignificant with respect to the delay through logic gates. In an FPGA, the routing is done through programmed muxes in the case of SRAM-based devices and through conducting vias in the case of antifuse devices. Both of these structures add significant delay to a signal. The muxes have a gate delay associated with them. The conducting vias have a high resistance, causing an RC delay. I discuss this in further detail in Section 3.5.

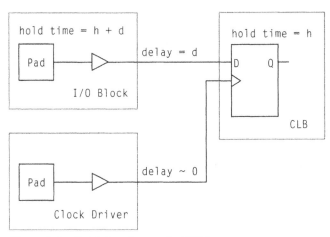

Figure 3.4   Hold time issues in FPGAs

Because of the large routing delays, if an input signal needed to be routed from an input buffer through internal interconnect to a flip-flop in a CLB inside the chip, as shown in Figure 3.4, there would be a large delay, labeled d, from the input pin to the data input of the flip-flop. In order to meet the hold time requirement of the internal flip-flop, labeled h, the hold time requirement for that signal with respect to the clock at the pins of the chip would be the sum of the delay d and hold time h which would be a large number and difficult to meet for devices interfacing with the FPGA. Instead, by placing flip-flops in the I/O blocks, the delay d is very small, resulting in a reasonable hold time at the pins of the chip.

Similarly, if an output needed to be routed from a flip-flop in a CLB inside the device directly to an output buffer, as shown in Figure 3.5, there would be a large delay from the flip-flop output to the pin of the chip. This means that the clock-to-output delay for all signals would be the delay of the flip-flop, labeled c, plus the delay of the routing, labeled d. All chips interfacing with the FPGA would need to have a very small setup time requirement, or the clock speed of the system would need to be reduced. The solution is to have the output flip-flop inside the I/O block so that it is right next to the buffers. Then the routing delay is not significant. Having input and output flip-flops in the I/O blocks allows the FPGA and the system in which it is designed to be as fast as possible.

Figure 3.5   Setup time issues in FPGAs

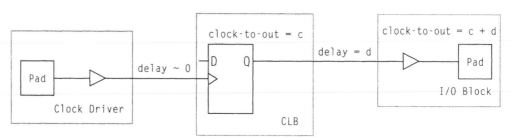

3.4 Embedded Devices

Many newer FPGA architectures are incorporating complex devices inside their FPGAs. These devices can range from relatively simple functions, such as address decoders or multipliers, all the way through ALUs, DSPs, and microcontrollers and microprocessors. These embedded devices are optimized, and the FPGA devices that include them can offer you a very nice way of integrating an entire system onto a single chip, creating what is being called a "system on a programmable chip" or SOPC.

The advantage of FPGAs with embedded devices is that you can save board area and power consumption. You can usually save cost and increase system speed with these FPGAs. The embedded devices are already tested, just like a standalone chip, so that you don't need to design the circuit from scratch and verify its functionality.

The disadvantage of these devices is that you tend to tie yourself into a single FPGA from a single FPGA vendor, losing some of the portability that engineers prefer. Each vendor has specific devices embedded into their FPGAs. In the case of embedded processors, each FPGA vendor usually licenses a specific processor core from a different processor manufacturer. This is good for the FPGA vendor because once they have a design win, that design is committed to their FPGA for some time. This is also a great way for the smaller FPGA vendors to differentiate themselves from the larger ones, by providing an embedded device that is in demand or soon will be, and can also produce a nice niche market for themselves that allows them to fend off eventual annihilation by the bigger vendors.

3.5 Programmable Interconnect

The interconnect of an FPGA is very different than that of a CPLD, but is rather similar to that of a gate array ASIC. Figure 3.6 shows the CLB's hierarchy of interconnect resources. Each CLB is connected with the immediately neighboring CLBs, as shown in the top left. These connections are sometimes called short lines. (Note that for simplicity only the connections with CLB1 in the top left are shown. In reality, all four CLBs have connections to their nearest neighbors. These connections allow logic that is too complex to fit into a single CLB to be mapped to multiple CLBs.)

Other routing resources consist of traces that pass by a number of CLBs before reaching switch matrices. These switch matrices allow a signal to be routed from one switch matrix to another to another, eventually connecting CLBs that can be relatively far from each other. The disadvantage to this method is that each trip through a switch matrix results in a significant delay. Often, in order to route signals through a chip, the routing delay becomes greater than the logic delay. This situation is unique to FPGAs and creates some of the design issues addressed in Chapter 5.

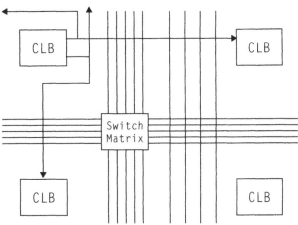

Figure 3.6   FPGA programmable interconnect (courtesy of Xilinx Inc.)

The third type of routing resource is the long line, which designers can use to connect critical CLBs that are physically far from each other on the chip without inducing much delay. These lines usually go from one end of the die to the other without connecting to a switch matrix. For critical path logic, long lines ensure that there will not be a significant delay.

The long line can also be used as buses within the chip. Three-state buffers are used to connect many CLBs to a long line, creating a bus. In an ASIC, three-state buses should be avoided because all three-state buses present a possible danger of contention or floating nodes, both of which can introduce long-term reliability problems if not designed carefully. Instead, muxes are used to combine many outputs because muxes are simple, easily expandable devices. In an ASIC, routing is not a significant problem. For an FPGA, though, muxes are not practical for connecting multiple outputs because this would require bringing outputs of different CLBs to a single CLB that contains the mux. Sometimes the CLBs producing the outputs are spread over a large section of the chip, requiring the signals to go through many switch matrices to reach the final destination. This introduces a very significant delay, slowing down the entire design.

Instead, CLBs near the long lines can directly drive the long lines with three-state drivers. The routing delay in this case is small. Of course, designers need to follow the techniques described in Chapter 5 carefully to avoid any bus contention or floating buses.

Figure 3.7 shows a more detailed view of the routing for a single CLB. Note that the CLB has connections to local interconnect to connect it to neighboring CLBs. Also, it uses muxes to drive outputs onto the longer interconnects to connect it to devices at other parts of the chip. In this particular architecture, inputs from the interconnects go directly into the CLB, where the logic determines whether to use or ignore these signals.

Note that CLBs themselves are often used for routing. In cases of high congestion on a chip, where routing resources are used up and not all signals and CLBs are connected, CLBs can be used for routing. In this case, the logic and muxes are set up so that a signal coming in simply goes out without any logical changes. This effectively increases routing resources in a densely packed design, but of course results in additional significant delay.

3.6 Clock Circuitry

Special I/O blocks with special high drive clock buffers, known as clock drivers, are distributed around the chip. These buffers are connected to clock input pins

Figure 3.7   CLB programmable interconnect (courtesy of Altera Corporation)

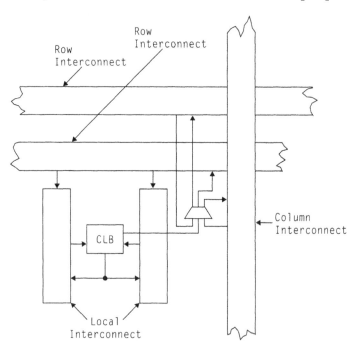

and drive the clock signals onto the global clock lines distributed throughout the device in a configuration called a clock tree. These clock lines are designed for low clock skew times and fast clock propagation times. As I discuss later, synchronous design is a must with FPGAs, because absolute skew times and delay times for signals cannot be guaranteed using the routing resources of the FPGA. Only when using clock signals from clock buffers can the relative delays and skew times be small and predictable.

3.7 SRAM vs. Antifuse Programming

There are two competing methods of programming FPGAs. The first, SRAM programming, involves static RAM bits as the programming elements. These bits can be combined in a single memory and used as a LUT to implement any kind of combinatorial logic, as described in Section 3.2. Also, programmers can use individual SRAM bits to control muxes, which select or deselect particular logic within a CLB, as described in Section 3.2. For routing, these bits can turn on a transistor that connects two traces in a switch matrix, or they can select the output of a mux that drives an interconnect line. Both methods are illustrated in Figure 3.8.

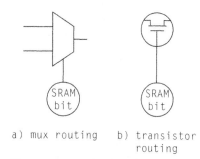

a) mux routing   b) transistor routing

Figure 3.8   FPGA routing using SRAM bits

The other programming method involves antifuses. A regular fuse normally makes a connection until an excessive amount of current goes through it, generating heat and breaking the connection. With an antifuse, there is a small link between two conductors that are separated by an insulator, as shown in Figure 3.9. When a large voltage is applied across the link, the link melts. As the link melts, the conductor material migrates across the link, creating a conducting path between the two conductors. This process is used to connect traces inside the FPGA.

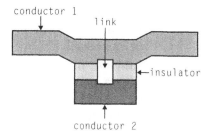

Figure 3.9   FPGA antifuses (courtesy of Quicklogic Corporation)

There are two main types of antifuses in production today. In one type, conductor 1 is polysilicon, and conductor 2 is n+ diffused silicon. The insulator is oxide-nitride-oxide (ONO) and the link is composed of silicon.

In the second type of antifuse, both conductors are metal, the insulator is amorphous silicon, and the link is composed of titanium or tungsten silicide.

SRAM-based FPGAs have the advantage of being reprogrammable. Especially as FPGAs become larger and therefore more expensive, it is a nice feature during debugging to be able to reprogram them rather than toss out a bad design. SRAM-based FPGAs can also be reprogrammed while in the system, which makes in-field upgrading very easy. Programmers can alter a communication protocol or add a feature to the FPGA by a simple software change. SRAM-based FPGAs allow you to include small memories like FIFOs in your design, though large memories inside an FPGA are not cost effective. Also, SRAM-based FPGAs can be used for reconfigurable computing, a concept whereby computers contain FPGAs and algorithms can be compiled to run in the FPGAs.

A disadvantage of SRAM-based FPGAs is that they're reprogrammable. Some applications, particularly military ones, often require that a device be non-volatile and not susceptible to changes from radiation or power glitches. Antifuse FPGAs fit these criteria.

In theory, antifuse FPGAs are much faster than SRAM FPGAs. This is because antifuse FPGAs have a real connection between conductors for routing traces, as opposed to the logic or transistors used in SRAM-based FPGAs. Although the antifuse connections have a high resistance and therefore some RC delay associated with them, this delay should be much lower than the delay in SRAM-based FPGAs. You'll notice that I use some wishy-washy terms here. The reason is that, in practice, antifuse FPGAs are not significantly faster than SRAM-based FPGAs, despite the theory. That's because every semiconductor company in the world knows how to make SRAMs. It's a standard product using a standard technology. Even companies that do not produce SRAMs often use SRAM structures to test their new processes because the structures are so regular and their performance is predicable. And because each semiconductor company is continually trying to improve its processes, they are always making faster and smaller SRAMs. On the other hand, only a small number of semiconductor companies, those manufacturing antifuse FPGAs, know how to make antifuses. There simply aren't as many people or companies at work attempting to improve the yields, size, and speed of antifuses. For this reason, from a practical point of view, the speed difference between the two technologies is, and will probably remain, fairly small.

Antifuse FPGAs do have the advantage of lower power over SRAM-based FPGAs. Antifuse FPGAs also have an intellectual property security advantage. By this I mean that SRAM-based FPGAs must always be programmed by an external device upon power-up. It's possible, then, for some unscrupulous engineer to copy your design simply by capturing the external bit stream. This engineer can then load the bit stream into any other FPGA, making a perfect copy of your design. Because an antifuse FPGA is programmed once, the program and the design are safe from prying eyes.

A newer technology that shows promise is flash-based FPGAs. These devices are essentially the same as SRAM-based devices, except that they use flash EPROM bits for programming. Flash EPROM bits tend to be small and fast. They are nonvolatile like antifuse, but reprogrammable like SRAM. Flash-based FPGA routing is shown in Figure 3.10.

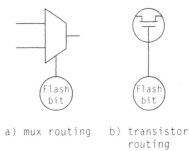

a) mux routing   b) transistor routing

Figure 3.10 FPGA routing using flash bits

Table 3.1 summarizes how SRAM and antifuse programming technologies compare.

Table 3.1   **Comparison of FPGA programming technologies.**

	SRAM	**Antifuse**
Volatile	Yes	No
In-system programmable	Yes	No
Speed	Fast	Somewhat faster
Power consumption	Higher	Lower
Density	High	High
IP security	No	Yes
Embedded RAM	Yes	No

3.8 Emulating and Prototyping ASICs

Designers can also use FPGAs in places where an ASIC will eventually be used. For example, designers may use an FPGA in a design that needs to get to market quickly at a low initial development cost. Later, they can replace the FPGA with an ASIC when the production volume increases, in order to reduce the part cost. Most FPGA designs, however, are not intended to be replaced by an ASIC.

Reconfigurable Computing

An interesting concept, reconfigurable computing, has been floating around universities for the past decade or so and has been the subject of a number of research papers. In recent years, some companies have begun offering different variations of the concept in actual products. Essentially, the concept behind configurable computing is that computations can be performed much faster using special purpose hardware than using general-purpose hardware (a processor) running software. Therefore, general computing could be sped up significantly if hardware could be dynamically reconfigured to act as a specialized coprocessors. Obviously, SRAM-based FPGAs would be an ideal implementation for this hardware.

The first, and most difficult, obstacle to reconfigurable computing is that a compiler must be able to partition a general-purpose computer program into software and hardware functionality by extracting the algorithms that can be implemented in hardware. It must then compile the algorithm code into an FPGA design. Synthesis programs have a difficult enough time doing the same operation using a hardware description language, which is designed specifically for this use. And a synthesis program doesn't need to partition the code between hardware and software — all of the HDL code represents hardware. Because the process is so difficult, synthesis programs restrict the HDL code to a specific coding style to make the job easier. Also, hardware designers still need to set switches within comments in the code and change settings of the synthesis program, in order to get usable results. And after all of this, the designer often needs to tweak the HDL code to fit the design into the FPGA and to meet the required performance criteria.

The second obstacle is the relatively long time required to load a new design into an FPGA. Unless companies can speed up this process, reconfigurable computing will be limited to algorithms that are repeated in a loop in the code, so that the overhead of reprogramming the FPGA is compensated by the number of times the hardware algorithm is executed.

As companies come to market with reconfigurable computing solutions, they have been taking a more practical approach than the "Holy Grail" described above. Some of the solutions include libraries of algorithms that have already been developed, tested, and synthesized and that can be called from software. Other companies have created new programming languages that combine the flexibility of C++, for example, with an HDL. Such languages make it easier for compilers to partition and synthesize the code. The disadvantage is that these a new non-standard languages represent a particularly challenging learning hurdle, becuase they require a knowledge of both software and hardware design techniques.

(Continued on page 47.)

FPGAs tend to be used where programmability, up-front cost, and time to market are more important than part cost, speed, or circuit density.

There are two methodologies in integrated circuit chip design where FPGAs are being used to assist in the development of chips and the development of software that depends on these chips. These methodologies are known as emulation and prototyping.

3.8.1   Emulation

Several companies provide standalone hardware boxes for emulating the function of an ASIC or a custom integrated circuit. These hardware emulators can be programmed with a design for a chip. Once programmed, the emulator can be physically connected to a target circuit board where the chip would normally be connected. Then, the entire target system can be run as if the chip were actually available and functioning. You can then debug the design using real world hardware and real world software. You can stop and start the hardware emulator in order to examine internal nodes of the design. You can capture waveform traces of internal and I/O signals for debugging. You can make changes to the design to correct mistakes or to improve performance, before the design is committed to silicon.

I believe that these practical, but limited solutions will eventually produce a real-world product that will have some use in specific areas. The progress of reconfigurable computing will probably parallel that of silicon compilation. In the early 1980s, some companies, such as Silicon Compilers, Inc., were touting the ability to go directly from a schematic diagram to a chip layout. The problem turned out to be bigger than these advocates thought; the algorithms needed were much more complex than they originally believed, and the computing power to execute the algorithms just wasn't available yet at a reasonable cost. So these companies all folded, but not without first producing corporate offspring and cousins, such as Synopsys Corporation, that decided they could tackle a much easier problem and still provide a solution that engineers could use. Their solution was software synthesis — software that could produce a gate level description from an RTL level description. This much less ambitious but much more achievable solution was a great success and may still eventually lead to the ultimate solution of silicon compilation. Many successful new products in the engineering design automation (EDA) industry follow this same trajectory. An ambitious first product fails, leading others to attempt smaller, less costly, more achievable products that succeed. In the same way, I believe, restricted solutions to reconfigurable computingwill make their way into the marketplace and be successful, and eventually lead to more and more complex implementations.

For example, if you are designing a new microprocessor, you could load the microprocessor design into a hardware emulator, plug the emulator into a target personal computer motherboard, and actually boot Linux or any other operating system. You could even run real applications. Of course, a hardware emulator runs at a fraction of the speed of the final chip, but it affords a form of testing that is otherwise not possible, except with prototyping.

Different hardware emulators from different manufacturers have different internal architectures. Many of them, though, use large sets of FPGAs to emulate the chip design, because FPGAs allow users to easily load and modify designs, stop the design while it is in the system, and easily examine internal nodes and external I/O.

3.8.2 Prototyping

As FPGAs become faster and denser, and ASICs become larger, prototyping has become an important alternative to emulation. Prototyping involves loading a chip design into one or more FPGAs. If the chip design fits into a single FPGA, the FPGA can be plugged into a socket or soldered into a target circuit board where the final chip will ultimately go. The board can then be powered up and tested using real data. If the design cannot fit into a single FPGA, a board can be designed that contains several FPGAs into which the chip design is partitioned. Companies now provide software that will automatically partition a chip design into multiple FPGAs.

These design-specific FPGA prototypes generally run faster than a hardware emulator because they do not have the overhead required for a general purpose machine, and there are fewer FPGAs — only the exact number required to implement your chip design. On the other hand, they do not have the built-in diagnostic capabilities of a hardware emulator, and they do not come with application engineers to support you. FPGA prototypes are generally cheaper than hardware emulators, but you must do all of the work, including partitioning the design, designing the board to hold the FPGAs, and designing whatever debug capabilities you require.

3.9 Summary

This section summarizes the various aspects of FPGAs that we have learned in this chapter. This section also provides a list of factors to use when deciding whether to choose a CPLD or FPGA for your design.

3.9.1 FPGA Selection Criteria

Knowledge of the internal architecture of FPGAs and the semiconductor technologies used to implement the programmable elements is critical for considering which FPGA to use in your design. When making that decision, you should take into account the following architectural and technological issues:

- Configurable logic blocks — Although most FPGAs have similar logic blocks, there are differences, for example, in the number of flip-flops and the width of the lookup tables. Try to find a CLB architecture that fits your design. If your design has wide combinatorial functions, choose an FPGA using CLBs with large numbers of inputs. If your design has many pipelined stages, you will prefer CLBs with several flip-flops. Newer architectures are always being developed that fit the needs of specific types of designs, such as digital signal processing.

- The number of CLBs in the device — This will determine how much logic the device can hold and how easily your design will fit into it.

- The number and type of I/O pins — Obviously, the FPGA will need to support the number of I/O pins in your design. Also, determine how many of these are general purpose I/O and how many are reserved for special functions such as clock input, master reset, etc.

- The number of clock input pins — Clock signals can be driven only into particular pins. If your design has several clock domains (i.e., sections driven by separate clocks), you will need an FPGA that has that many clock input pins.

- Embedded devices — Does your design interface with devices such as a microcontroller or a PLL? Many FPGAs now incorporate specialized functions like these, which will make your job much easier and allow you to integrate more devices into a single FPGA.

- Antifuse vs. SRAM programming — Which technology makes sense for your design? Do you need the speed, low power, nonvolatility, and security of an antifuse device, or do you need the reprogrammability of an SRAM-based device?

- Emulating and prototyping ASICs — FPGAs can be found in off-the-shelf hardware emulators for testing the design of an ASIC in a real-world target before it goes to silicon. Or you can use FPGAs to create your own custom prototype of an ASIC for the same kind of pre-silicon real-world testing.

Other issues must be taken into account for all programmable chips that you intend to use in your design. For a list of these general issues, refer to Section 4.2 about the chip specification.

3.9.2   Choosing Between CPLDs and FPGAs

Choosing between a CPLD and an FPGA will depend on the requirements of your project. Table 3.2 shows a summary of the characteristics of each type of programmable device. You will notice that I use fuzzy terms like "low," "medium," and "high" for some of the characteristics. People often want me to give a definitive answer on, for example, the number of gates in a typical CPLD or the cost of a typical FPGA. Because these numbers change so quickly, they are wrong as soon as they leave my lips (or in this case when they reach print). For that reason, I prefer to give relative characteristics that will still be correct for a while after I give them.

Table 3.2   CPLDs vs. FPGAs

	CPLD	FPGA
Architecture	PAL-like	Gate array–like
Speed	Fast, predictable	Application dependent
Density	Low to medium	Medium to high
Interconnect	Crossbar	Routing
Power consumption	High per gate	Low per gate

Exercises

1. What does the term FPGA mean?
   (a) Formally Programmable Gate Array
   (b) Field Programmable Gate Array
   (c) Finite Programmable Gate Array

2. Select all of the parts of a typical FPGA architecture.
   (a) Configurable logic blocks
   (b) Configurable program blocks
   (c) Programmable interconnect
   (d) Configurable I/O blocks
   (e) Programmable address decode blocks

3. Select TRUE or FALSE for the following statements:
   (a) TRUE or FALSE: Configurable I/O blocks contain flip-flops on the inputs to enable a designer to reduce the hold-time requirement for the inputs.
   (b) TRUE or FALSE: Configurable I/O blocks contain flip-flops on the outputs to enable the designer to decrease the clock-to-output times of the outputs.
   (c) TRUE or FALSE: FPGA programmable interconnect consists of lines that start at one end of the chip and continue to the other end to enable all CLBs to be connected.
   (d) TRUE or FALSE: Programmable switches inside the chip allow the connection of CLBs to interconnect lines.
   (e) TRUE or FALSE: Programmable switches inside the chip allow the connection of interconnect lines to each other and to the switch matrix.
   (f) TRUE or FALSE: Each flip-flop in an FPGA has its own unique clock line and clock buffer to reduce skew.
   (g) TRUE or FALSE: Any input to an FPGA can be used for the clock input.
   (h) TRUE or FALSE: Antifuse FPGAs use an industry standard process.
   (i) TRUE or FALSE: Antifuse technology is faster than SRAM technology, in theory.
   (j) TRUE or FALSE: SRAM FPGAs are more common than antifuse FPGAs.

4. Select all potential advantages of embedded devices
   (a) Reduced board area
   (b) Reduced power consumption
   (c) Reduced cost
   (d) Increased system speed
   (e) No need to design and test the embedded device

5. Select TRUE or FALSE for each of the following statements about SRAM-based FPGAs and antifuse FPGAs:
   (a) SRAM-based FPGAs are based on an industry standard technology.
   (b) In theory, SRAM-based FPGAs are much slower than antifuse FPGAs.
   (c) Antifuse FPGAs retain their programming after being powered off and then on again.
   (d) Antifuse FPGAs can be erased and reprogrammed.
   (e) SRAM-based FPGAs can be erased and reprogrammed.
   (f) In practice, SRAM-based FPGAs are much slower than antifuse FPGAs.
   (g) SRAM-based FPGAs are programmed using high voltages.
   (h) Antifuse FPGAs are programmed using high voltages.

6. Clock trees are designed for (select one)
   (a) Low speed and low power
   (b) Small delay and low power
   (c) Small delay and low skew
   (d) Low inductance and low skew
   (e) Low power and high density

7. Fill in the following table by selecting the correct attributes of CPLDs and FPGAs from the choices in each box.

	CPLD	FPGA
Architecture	Gate array–like PAL-like PROM-like	Gate array–like PAL-like PROM-like
Density	Low to medium Medium to high	Low to medium Medium to high
Speed	Fast and predictable Slow and predictable Application dependent	Fast and predictable Slow and predictable Application dependent
Interconnect	Bonded Routing Crossbar	Bonded Routing Crossbar
Power consumption	Negligible Low per gate High per gate	Negligible Low per gate High per gate

In this chapter...

- *UDM and UDM-PD*
- *Specification and specification review*
- *Devices and tools*
- *Design, simulate, and review*
- *Testing*

Chapter 4

Universal Design Methodology for Programmable Devices (UDM-PD)

This chapter describes the Universal Design Methodology for programmable devices. This method, based on my years of experience designing many types of programmable devices for small and large companies in different industries, lays out the entire process for designing a programmable device. Following the UDM guarantees that you will not overlook any steps and that you will have the best chance of creating a chip that functions correctly in your system.

Objectives

In this chapter, using Universal Design Methodology as a reference model, you will learn what steps are necessary to create working, reliable chips that function correctly in your system. The first section of this chapter explains UDM and specifically UDM-PD for programmable devices. The following sections detail each step of the design process and how it relates to the method. Reading this chapter will help you:

- Understand the UDM and UDM-PD methods.

- Discover the importance of writing a specification and performing a specification review.
- Learn how to choose appropriate programmable devices and software tools based on your specification.
- Recognize the issues to consider when synthesizing your design.
- Understand the need for proper simulation, review, and testing techniques during and after the process.

4.1 What is UDM and UDM-PD?

After years of designing circuit boards, ASICs, FPGAs, and CPLDs for a large number of companies, I noticed that engineers rarely followed a complete methodology, i.e., a complete set of standard procedures and steps. In many cases, companies simply assumed their engineers somehow knew what to do next — and the outstanding engineers often did. If the methodology was in some brilliant engineer's head, though, when that engineer left the company the methodology left, too, leaving the company to rediscover and redevelop the knowledge through costly trial-and-error. In those companies that had established procedures, the process documentation often consisted of scattered notes and files; rarely was the documentation compiled in one place.

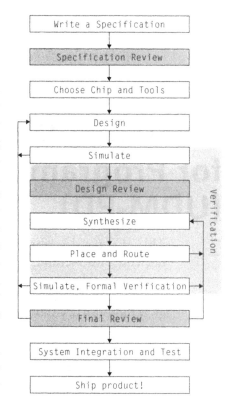

Even in companies that followed a defined procedure, often parts of the procedure were not well understood or completely implemented. For example, a company might emphasize the design process and not understand the testing process.

Figure 4.1   Design Flow

Eventually, as a consultant going from company to company, I decided I needed a methodology that I could take with me for each new design. It would have to be one that applied universally to large and small companies in any industry. Rather than being a method that described very specific steps, it would need to be a methodology that could be generally applied to different designs. I called this methodology the Universal Design Methodology. As technology changed, the methodology was adapted. I did find that different types of devices required slightly different methodologies. ASICs and printed circuit boards required slightly different methodologies than FPGAs and CPLDs. The methodology described here is specifically for programmable devices, and I call it UDM-PD.

4.1.1 The Goals of UDM

The goals of the Universal Design Methodology are these:

- Design a device that
- Is free from manufacturing defects
- Works reliably over the lifetime of the device
- Functions correctly in your system
- Design this device efficiently, meaning
- In the least amount of time
- Using the least amount of resources, including personnel
- Plan the design efficiently, meaning
- Create a reasonable schedule as early in the process as possible
- Know all necessary resources up front and allocate them as early in the process as possible

4.1.2 The Design Flow of UDM-PD

UDM-PD specifies a design flow that enables you to reach the UDM design goals when designing a programmable device. The design flow consists of the steps shown in Figure 4.1. Each particular design will have slight variations in the specifics of each step, but essentially the steps will be the same. By understanding the entire flow before the project begins, you will be able to meet goal number three, a better understanding of how to schedule and allocate resources for the development process.

4.2 Writing a Specification

I cannot overstate the importance of a specification. A specification is an absolute must, especially as a guide for choosing the right device and the right technology and for making your needs known to the vendor. All too often I've been called in to consult for a company, and when I ask to see the spec, I am told that it doesn't exist. Or I am given a copy of a spec, but told to ignore it because it is not up to date.

A specification allows each engineer to understand the entire design and his piece of it. It allows the engineer to design the correct interface to the rest of the chip. It also saves time and thus cost, and helps avoid misunderstanding. There is no excuse for not having a written specification.

A specification should include the following information:

- External block diagram showing how the chip fits into the system
- Internal block diagram showing each major functional section
- Description of the I/O pins, including:
  - Output drive capability
  - Input threshold level (e.g., CMOS, TTL, ECL, etc.)
- Timing estimates, including:
  - Setup and hold times for input pins
  - Propagation times for output pins
  - Clock cycle time
- Gate count estimate
- Package type
- Power consumption target
- Price target
- Test procedures

It is very important to understand that the specification is a living document. Many sections will have best guesses in them, but these will become more accurate as the chip is being designed. Engineering problems will arise that will require compromises in functionality. Market changes may require changes in the specification. All of these decisions must use the specification as an up-to-date reference and all subsequent changes must be entered into the specification.

4.2.1 External Block Diagram

The external block diagram must show how the device fits into the system. This diagram will help describe the overall functionality of the device and will be a good reference for the system designers, PC board designers, designers of other chips in the system, and software developers.

4.2.2 Internal Block Diagram

The internal block diagram will be the starting point for the behavioral description of the device. As the behavioral HDL code changes, these changes must be incorporated into the internal block diagram. As other factors necessitate changes in the internal block diagram, these changes can also be incorporated easily into the behavioral HDL code.

4.2.3   Description of the I/O Pins

The device that you choose is often restricted by the requirements of the I/O pins. The number of pins will help decide which package you will need. The electrical characteristics of the I/O will determine which vendors and which technologies can be used.

Life Without Specification

One of my first jobs out of school was at a large semiconductor company. Although this company had developed some unique analog parts and a few digital parts in its history, the company was known mostly for second sourcing "jelly beans." That was the term for high volume, small density parts such as TTL logic. They were able to crank them out in volume at cut-rate prices. To their credit, they saw the future of high-end microprocessors and microprocessor peripherals that had much lower volumes but much higher profit margins. What they didn't understand was that these parts were much more complex and that they accordingly required more sophisticated design methods and procedures to produce. Instead, the engineers, project leaders, and managers at this company continued to use the same old procedures that they had for the small jellybean parts.

The inability to recognize the need for better procedures and methodologies really doomed this company to failure over the next decade. When other companies, like Intel, were rising to dominance, this company's revenues had a steady decline, and it was eventually bought by a much larger company.

One example of this shortsightedness was with regard to specifications. I was recruited out of college to join the microprocessor group, which had the mandate to create complex peripheral devices, such as memory managers and cache controllers, for the Motorola family of processors. Typically, two or three of the best engineers in the department were assigned to a single chip. The entire documentation for the chip consisted of handfuls of schematics and lab books with handwritten notes.

Without the necessary direction or planning that these large designs required, they often dragged on, missing schedule after schedule. Eventually, these engineers would leave the company, frustrated at not being able to get their designs out the door. Each time this happened, there was no specification to turn to. It was impossible to bring a new engineer onto the project because one third or one half of the entire specification had walked out the door in the head of the engineer who had left. I saw all four major chip designs in this division die for exactly these reasons. Eventually, without a single significant product in over two years, the division was closed down.

A Living Document

My last full-time employer (before becoming a full-time consultant) was a telecom startup. The company had lots of problems and became a great example of what not to do when designing a product or running a company.

One of these problems should have been an early warning sign for me. I joined the company as the main ASIC designer–employee number nine and the only one with any experience designing chips. One of the chips that needed to be designed was a simple buffer between a board and a backplane. The logic requirements of the design were extremely simple, but the current drive requirements — 48 mA per signal for 8 signals — was more than most ASIC vendors could produce at the time. We found that one company, NCR Corporation, had the technology. Because the logic design was so simple, we decided that I would produce a written specification that would be handed off to the engineers at NCR. I would supervise their progress while I did the real design work on another important chip.

At the end of the design review, one of the engineers at the company adamantly stated that we should demand that NCR meet the specifications that we had written. If not, he proclaimed, we would not pay them. That would give them the incentive they needed to design the chip to our specifications. I said that it made more sense for us to work with them to understand any issues that might arise. If NCR couldn't meet the specification, we would work with them to get the best results possible and see how we could change the specifications, and the specifications of our system, to get the best results possible. He was insistent. We argued for some time, the other engineers at the review sitting quietly and uncomfortably. Finally, I told him that I agreed. If NCR couldn't manufacture the chip, we should refuse to pay them. We would then save the $20,000 NRE fee. He smiled. I then said that we could all go home because we had saved all that money, had no chips for our boards, no working product, no company, and no jobs. I think I then called him an idiot.

Luckily the president of this company saw my logic immediately and agreed that we should work with NCR to produce the best product that we could. If, along the way the specifications needed to be changed, we would change them. The written specification is not gospel; it's a living, changing roadmap that gets you where you're going even if a lightning storm suddenly throws a tree along the road. You must be specific enough to create your design, and flexible enough to make changes when necessary.

And by the way, don't call anyone an idiot at a company meeting, even if it's true. It makes an enemy for a long time — an enemy who can take revenge in secret ways, refuse to cooperate on important projects, and blame you for all of his mistakes. I'm speaking from experience.

4.2.4 Timing Estimates

Timing estimates are needed to determine which devices, vendors, and technologies can be used. You should have a good understanding of the clock frequency required for the design and also the setup and hold time requirements of the I/O. (These requirements are determined by the interface between your device and the other chips in the system.)

Remember to identify all asynchronous input signals. You can then discuss metastability issues with the vendors that you are considering. This will give you an idea about how well the vendor has characterized their devices and the technical proficiency of their own engineers — a definite factor in choosing a vendor.

4.2.5 Gate Count Estimate

As you gain experience designing programmable devices, estimating gate counts will become easier. For your first few designs, talk to the various vendors you are considering. They will be able to help you construct reasonable estimates and determine which of their devices are appropriate for your design.

4.2.6 Package Type

Package type is often a very large percentage of the entire cost of an FPGA. Understand the package options offered by different vendors. Also, you will need to understand the capabilities of your PC board layout designers and fabrication facilities to work with the different package types.

4.2.7 Power Consumption Target

Be certain you understand the variables that affect the device's power consumption. You must also understand how the device's operation will affect overall board and system power consumption. Finally, whoever is designing or choosing the power supply will need to know how much power, typical case and worst case, each chip in the system will require.

4.2.8 Price Target

For most projects, you will need a realistic price target. This target can help you determine the necessary tradeoffs between pin count, functionality, speed, package type, and other factors.

4.2.9 Test Procedures

Test procedures must be known at a very early stage of the design flow. Too often, design teams leave test procedures for the end of the design flow at which time they discover that the device cannot be tested completely or accurately. If the tests require software, the software team must begin planning the tests very

The Correct Way To Calculate Power Consumption

Engineers often ask me about power calculations for circuit boards or systems. When they add up the worst-case power consumption numbers for all of the parts in the system, they end up with a number so large that it seems unreasonable. They can't justify designing in a power supply that large, or the necessary cooling needed to get the predicted temperature down to something acceptable. When they put the system together, the power numbers are often much closer to the typical power consumption numbers than the worst-case power consumption numbers. Many engineers simply shrug or apply some rule of thumb such as cutting the worst-case power number by a factor of two. Some engineers are bothered by the fact that the numbers are off. Some know the secret to correctly calculating worst-case power consumption, and I'm about to reveal that secret to you.

The power numbers which manufacturer's report for individual components are statistical numbers. The best case and worst case numbers are usually values three sigma in either direction from the mean (looking at a standard Bell curve). In other words, there is an insignificant probability that the power consumption is more than the worst-case numbers or less than the best-case numbers. If you treat the individual components statistically, you should treat the entire circuit board or system statistically.

Therefore, to get a realistic number of the best-case, typical-case, and worst-case power consumption for a system, use the following formulae (which are standard formulae for the mean and standard deviation of a discrete random variable):

Minimum system power $P_{min} = \sum P_{i,\,typ} - \sqrt{\sum (P_{i,\,typ} - P_{i,\,min})^2}$

Typical system power $P_{typ} = \sum P_{i,\,typ}$

Maximum system power $P_{max} = \sum P_{i,\,typ} + \sqrt{\sum (P_{i,\,max} - P_{i,\,typ})^2}$

where

$P_{i,\,min}$ is the minimum power of component i

$P_{i,\,typ}$ is the typical power of component i

$P_{i,\,max}$ is the maximum power of component i

Using the formula for worst-case maximum power consumption of a system, you'll find that the more components in the system, the closer this maximum power is to the typical power. And this makes sense. For a system with many components, it is more likely that most of them are running under typical conditions and only a few of them are running at worst-case conditions.

early, and they must have input into the hardware design so that testability is built in from the beginning.

4.3 Specification Review

At the end of the specification phase, it is very important to have a design review. As many people as are interested should take part in this review, because this specification is the basis for the entire chip. You want to know right now if anything is wrong or has been left out. Invite people from all departments who are specifically involved with the chip and the system, including marketing, sales, software, applications, etc.

4.4 Choosing Device and Tools

Once a specification has been written, the design team can use it to find the best vendor with a technology and price structure that best meets their requirements. They can also choose tools to work well together and with the device and technology they have chosen.

One important case in point for choosing the device and tools at this early stage is that of synthesis. The selection of a synthesis tool will determine the coding style for the RTL HDL. A specific coding style is necessary because synthesis tools cannot do a good job if they must handle too many code possibilities. For example, there are many ways to code state machines. If the synthesis tool needs to understand each possible way, it becomes more complex and thus more error prone. To avoid problems like this, synthesis tool vendors specify coding guidelines guaranteeing that their tools will recognize the structures you are designing and synthesize them correctly to gate level descriptions.

4.5 Design

When designing the chip, remember to design according to the rules that are discussed in detail in Chapter 5. These are

- Use top-down design
- Work with the device architecture
- Do synchronous design
- Protect against metastability
- Avoid floating nodes
- Avoid bus contention

A Testing Horror Story

If you're frightened easily, don't read further. Some years ago I was called into a small startup company that was designing medical imaging equipment. The founder of the company, an engineer, had been kicked out by the investors. The senior members of the engineering team, maybe three or four people, left with him. The company called me in as a consultant to help them figure out why the hardware they had didn't work. Through a painful reverse engineering process (the fleeing engineers had left no documentation), I found a slew of reliability problems that I corrected one by one. At that point, although we had a working board covered by blue wires, I suggested that we redesign the board. The company agreed. I then submitted a plan, including a test plan, whereby the software engineers would write code to test the hardware.

When the board had been redesigned and it came back from fabrication and assembly, I went to the software engineers to get the code to begin testing. The software engineers told me that the new Vice President of Engineering had changed all of the priorities so that the test code was dead last on the list.

I went to the VP's office for an explanation. He explained that getting the next round of funding was contingent on getting a beta site for our system. If we had a system working in a hospital, then we could get funding to keep going. Otherwise the company would be out of business. How could we get the system working, I asked, if we couldn't test the hardware. Wouldn't it be better if we put a working system into a beta site than a nonworking one? He told me that he trusted my abilities so much that he was sure my hardware worked perfectly. I told him that I appreciated his confidence, but even I don't deserve that kind of responsibility.

The story gets worse. I decided to write some software tests at that time. It was difficult because I didn't understand all of the software running on this system. I was able to get a test running that looped random data throughout this imaging system. Lo and behold, sometimes the data sent out came back corrupted. I showed this to the VP and to the CEO of the company. Their response? Don't worry. It's only a few pixels that get corrupted. No one will miss them. What if these pixels were enough to look like a tumor to a doctor reviewing the image, I asked. Or worse, God forbid, they covered up a real tumor? Don't worry, was the reply I got again. We'll fix it after we get the funding.

I finished up my work at the company, collected my check, and left when the contract expired. A year later they had been turned down for more funding and went out of business.

4.6 Verification

Verification is a "super-phase" because it consists of several other phases of the design process. Which exact phases that make up verification is open to argument, but generally verification can be broken into several phases, each of which is essential to the entire process. These steps consist of

- Simulation
- Design review
- Synthesis
- Place and route
- Formal verification

The components of verification are discussed further in the following sections and in much greater detail in Chapter 6.

4.6.1   Simulation

Simulation is an ongoing process; some kind of simulation will be performed as part of nearly every stage of the design process. Small sections of the design should be simulated separately before hooking them up to larger sections, as described in Chapter 7. There will be many iterations of design and simulation in order to get the correct functionality.

4.6.2   Design Review

Once design and simulation are finished, another design review must take place so that other engineers can check the design. It is important to get other engineers to look over the simulations. At this stage, they should be looking for missed details and improper assumptions. This is one of the most important reviews because only with correct and complete simulation will you know that the chip will work correctly in your system.

In addition to the chip design team, you should invite engineers who were not involved in the actual chip design to this review. Often, the chip designers will inadvertently make assumptions that outsiders would question. These outsiders can also suggest corner cases that were not already simulated that will often uncover additional problems in the design.

4.6.3   Synthesis

The next step is to synthesize the chip. This involves using synthesis software to optimally translate your RTL design into a gate level design that can be mapped to logic blocks in the FPGA. This may involve specifying switches and optimization criteria in the HDL code, or playing with parameters of the synthesis software in order to ensure good timing and utilization.

After synthesis, the chip must be resimulated using the gate level output of the synthesis tool. If everything has gone well up to this point, the gate level simulation results will agree with the RTL results. Another possibility is to use a formal verification tool that will logically compare the RTL description to the gate level description. Whichever method is used, the design team will need to address any discrepancies. Discrepancies discovered at this stage often are the result of processing RTL code that doesn't conform to the style rules expected

The Need For Specification Reviews

After about two years at the large semiconductor company that employed me right out of school, I was given my first responsibility as a project leader designing a dual universal asynchronous receiver transmitter, or dual UART. I had another engineer reporting to me, and I was pretty excited about this. The project had some visibility within the division and people would periodically stop me to find out about my progress. What confused me, though, was that different people from different departments had different ideas about what I was designing. One day, a sales person would ask me about the quad UART. I would explain that it was a dual UART. They would say something about customers needing four, not two, on a chip. Another day, a marketing person would ask me about the UART. I would explain that it was a dual UART. They would say something about the customers who had been waiting for a UART to drop into their existing systems. When I mentioned a quad UART to the people in semiconductor processing, they would laugh, saying it wasn't possible to put a device that large on a single die and still fit into an existing package.

I finally decided to hold a specification review — something that I then realized should have been held at the beginning of the project. I invited the managers from engineering, sales, marketing, testing, and production. In going over the specifications I found that the product I was in charge of met no one's expectations and could probably not be sold. Had we known this at the beginning, we could have modified the specifications or spent our energies on a product that would actually make money.

Afterwards, I was told to continue working on the chip, despite the fact that we couldn't sell it, because we had already announced it and wanted to show that at least once we could produce something we had publicized. Demoralized about my new project, I continued with the company long enough to get the chip design on the right track and put it in the hands of my colleague. The design was fully documented, a rarity at this company, and I left to find other work. Later I found out that the design was cancelled right before production because someone higher up found out that no one really wanted to buy it.

by the synthesis tool. Correcting these problems is usually a straightforward matter of rewriting the code in the correct format.

4.6.4 Place and Route

The next step is to lay out the chip, resulting in a real layout for a real chip. This involves using the vendor's software tools to place various functions into the available blocks in the device and to route the blocks together. The software will figure out the bits needed to program the chip to implement the design. If you cannot successfully place the design into the device and route it, you may need to tweak the design. In some cases, you will need to make radical changes, such as eliminating some functionality or using a larger device. If you have followed all of the procedures outlined in this book, the chances of a major problem at this stage, resulting in a major design change, will be minimized.

Once the place and route is successful, the design team must perform timing analysis. The timing analysis will determine whether the design meets the timing goals. Typically, the design team will need to redesign and resimulate certain paths in order to get the correct timing. In some cases, they will need to change functionality, or they will need to change the timing specifications of the chip, in order to get the design to work.

4.6.5 Resimulation and Formal Verification

At this stage, the design team must check the results of synthesis to make sure that the RTL design that was fully simulated is functionally equivalent to the gate level design that was produced after synthesis. In some cases, it may also be necessary to show that the configuration of the programmable device behaves identically to the RTL description. There are two ways to do this: by resimulating the lower level design or by using formal verification. In some cases, both techniques can be used for further certainty.

Resimulation

The most common method of determining that the input circuit and the final circuit are correct is to resimulate the final circuit using all of the tests that were used to simulate the original circuit. These tests are called *regression tests*. The results of both circuits should be identical for each clock edge.

Equivalency Checking

The formal verification that takes place at this stage is known as *equivalency checking*. This kind of formal verification involves a software tool that compares the RTL design with the gate level design created by the synthesis software, or possibly even compares it with the resulting configuration of the FPGA or CPLD. This software performs a mathematical comparison of the functionality of both circuits in order to confirm that both circuits will operate correctly.

4.7 Final Review

The final review of the chip should be a formality at this point. If the design team has followed all of the other steps and the other reviews have taken place, this review should be a simple sign-off that verifies that the design has been coded, simulated, synthesized, laid out and routed, and is now ready to go into the system.

4.8 System Integration and Test

For a one-time programmable device such as most CPLDs or an antifuse FPGA, you simply program the device at this time, and you immediately have your prototypes. For a reprogrammable chip, such as an SRAM-based FPGA, you place a blank chip into your system, and the system programs it during power up. In either case, you have the responsibility to determine that the entire system, with your programmable device, actually works correctly.

If you have followed the procedure up to this point, chances are very good that your system will perform correctly with only minor problems. The design team can often work around these minor problems by modifying the system or changing the system software. The team needs to test and document these problems so that they can fix them on the next revision of the chip. System integration and system testing is necessary at this point to ensure that all parts of the system work correctly together.

When the chips are put into production, the production process should include some sort of burn-in test that continually tests the system over some long amount of time. If a chip has been designed correctly, it will only fail because of marginal physical defects that will usually show up with this kind of stress testing.

4.9 Ship Product!

At this point you are done. It is time to ship your product and take that long awaited vacation.

4.10 Summary

The Universal Design Methodology as it relates specifically to programmable devices ensures the proper design, review, and testing of your product. This methodology, called UDM-PD, has the following goals:

1. Design a device that
   - is free from manufacturing defects
   - works reliably over the lifetime of the device
   - functions correctly in your system
2. Design this device efficiently, meaning
   - in the least amount of time
   - using the least amount of resources, including personnel
3. Plan the design efficiently, meaning
   - create a reasonable schedule as early in the process as possible
   - know all necessary resources up front and allocate them as early in the process as possible

In this chapter, we have also studied the design flow that is associated with UDM-PD. This design flow has the following stages:

- Writing a specification
- A specification review
- Choosing programmable devices and software tools
- Designing the chip
- Simulating the design
- Design review
- Synthesizing the design
- Place and route of the design
- Resimulation and/or formal verification
- Final review
- Testing the chip
- Integrating the chip into the system and testing the system
- Shipping the product

Exercises

1. Select the three major goals of UDM-PD.
   - (a) Design the device efficiently
   - (b) Design a device synchronously
   - (c) Plan to design a device
   - (d) Design a device that works reliably over the lifetime of the device
   - (e) Allocate a maximum number of resources in the minimum amount of time
   - (f) Plan the design efficiently

2. UDM is a methodology to design a device that (choose all that apply)
   - (a) Is free from manufacturing defects
   - (b) Can be tested automatically
   - (c) Functions correctly in your system
   - (d) Works reliably over the lifetime of the device
   - (e) Is inexpensive

3. UDM is a methodology to design a device efficiently, meaning (choose all that apply)
   - (a) In the least amount of time
   - (b) Using the least number of people
   - (c) Using the least amount of resources

4. UDM is a methodology to plan a design efficiently, meaning (choose all that apply)
   - (a) Writing a specification that will not change
   - (b) Knowing all necessary resources up front and allocating them as early in the process as possible
   - (c) Creating a reasonable schedule as early in the process as possible
   - (d) Planning to ship products while testing the design

5. Put each phase of the design flow in the correct order.
   - (a) Ship product!
   - (b) System integration and test
   - (c) Write a specification
   - (d) Final review
   - (e) Specification review

(f) Resimulation

(g) Choose device and tools

(h) Simulate

(i) Place and route

(j) Design review

(k) Design

(l) Synthesis

6. A design specification should include the following (select all that apply):

(a) The name of the FPGA vendor

(b) A description of the I/O pins, including output drive capabilities and input threshold levels

(c) The estimated gate count

(d) The target power consumption

(e) Test procedures, including in-system test requirements

(f) An external block diagram showing how the FPGA fits into the system

(g) A notice that the document, once approved, cannot be changed

(h) An internal block diagram showing each major functional section

(i) Timing estimates, including setup and hold times for input pins, propagation times for output pins, and the clock cycle time

(j) The target price

(k) The package type

In this chapter...

- *Hardware description languages*
- *Top-down design*
- *Synchronous design*
- *Floating nodes*
- *Bus contention*
- *Design for test (DFT)*
- *Built-in self-test (BIST)*
- *Signature analysis*

Chapter 5

Design Techniques, Rules, and Guidelines

This chapter presents design techniques, rules, and guidelines that are critical to FPGA and CPLD design. By understanding these concepts, you increase your chances of producing a working, reliable device that will work for different chip vendor processes and continue to work for the lifetime of your system.

In certain sections of this chapter, I show a number of examples of incorrect or inefficient designs, and the equivalent function designed correctly. I assume that you are using, or will be using, a hardware description language (HDL) like Verilog or VHDL to design your CPLD or FPGA. Most, if not all CPLDs and FPGAs are designed using HDLs. This chapter presents these design examples using schematics, but I also give the equivalent Verilog code for many of these circuits in Appendix B. Although HDLs are much more efficient for creating large designs, schematics are still preferred for illustrating small designs because they give a nice visual representation of what is going on.

Note that EDA tools that enable many of the techniques in this chapter are described in detail in Chapter 7.

Objectives

This chapter focuses on the potential problems that an engineer must recognize when designing an FPGA or CPLD and the design techniques that are used to avoid these problems. More specifically, reading this chapter will help you:

- Learn the fundamental concepts of hardware description languages.
- Appreciate the process of top-down design and how it is used to organize a design and speed up the development time.
- Comprehend how FPGA and CPLD architecture and internal structures affect your design.
- Understand the concept of synchronous design, know how to spot asynchronous circuits, and how to redesign an asynchronous circuit to be synchronous.
- Recognize what problems floating internal nodes can cause and learn how to avoid these problems.
- Understand the consequences of bus contention and techniques for avoiding it.
- Comprehend one-hot state encoding for optimally creating state machines in FPGAs.
- Design testability into a circuit from the beginning and understand various testability structures that are available.

5.1 Hardware Description Languages

Design teams can use a hardware description language to design at any level of abstraction, from high level architectural models to low-level switch models. These levels, from least amount of detail to most amount of detail are as follows:

- Behavioral models
  - Algorithmic
  - Architectural
- Structural models
  - Register Transfer Level (RTL)
  - Gate level
  - Switch level

These levels refer to the types of models that are used to represent a circuit design. The top two levels use what are called behavioral models, whereas the lower three levels use what are called structural models. Behavioral models consist of code that represents the behavior of the hardware without respect to its actual implementation. Behavioral models don't include timing numbers. Buses don't need to be broken down into their individual signals. Adders can simply add two or more numbers without specifying registers or gates or transistors. The two types of behavioral models are called algorithmic models and architectural models.

Algorithmic models simply represent algorithms that act on data. No hardware implementation is implied in an algorithmic model. So an algorithmic model is similar to what a programmer might write in C or Java to describe a function. The algorithmic model is coded to be fast, efficient, and mathematically correct. An algorithmic model of a circuit can be simulated to test that the basic specification of the design is correct.

Architectural models specify the blocks that implement the algorithms. Architectural models may be divided into blocks representing PC boards, ASICs, FPGAs, or other major hardware components of the system, but they do not specify how the algorithms are implemented in each particular block. These models of a circuit can be compared to an algorithmic model of the same circuit to discover if a chip's architecture is correctly implementing the algorithm. The design team can simulate the algorithmic model to find bottlenecks and inefficiencies before any of the low level design has begun.

Some sample behavioral level HDL code is shown in Listing 5.1. This sample shows a multiplier for two unsigned numbers of any bit width. Notice the very high level of description — there are no references to gates or clock signals.

Listing 5.1   Sample behavioral level HDL code

```
// ********************************************************
// ***** Multiplier for two unsigned numbers *****
// ********************************************************
// Look for the multiply enable signal
always @(posedge multiply_en) begin
    product <= a*b;
end
```

Structural models consist of code that represents specific pieces of hardware. RTL specifies the logic on a register level. In other words, the simplest RTL code specifies register logic. Actual gates are avoided, although RTL code may use Boolean functions that can be implemented in gates. The example RTL code in Listing 5.2 shows a multiplier for two unsigned 4-bit numbers. This level is the level at which most digital design is done.

Listing 5.2   Sample RTL HDL code

```
// ********************************************************
// ***** Multiplier for two unsigned 4-bit numbers *****
// ********************************************************


                                        // Look at the rising edge of the clock
always @(posedge clk) begin
        if (multiply_en == 1) begin        // Set up the multiplication
            count <= ~0;                   // Set count to its max value
            product <= 0;                  // Zero the product
        end


        if (count) begin
            if (b[count]) begin
                                           // If this bit of the multiplier is 1, shift
                                           // the product left and add the multiplicand
                product <= (product << 1) + a;
            end
            else begin
                                           // If this bit of the multiplier is 0,
                                           // just shift the product left
                product <= product << 1;
            end

            count <= count - 1;            // Decrement the count
        end
end
```

Gate level modeling consists of code that specifies gates such as NAND and NOR gates (Listing 5.3) Gate level code is often the output of a synthesis program that reads the RTL level code that an engineer has used to design a chip and writes the gate level equivalent. This gate level code can then be optimized for placement and routing within the CPLD or FPGA. The code in Listing 5.3 shows the synthesized 4-bit unsigned multiplier where the logic has been mapped to individual CLBs of an FPGA. Notice that at this level all logic must be described in primitive functions that map directly to the CLB logic, making the code much longer.

(In fact, much of the code was removed for clarity. Buffers used to route signals and the Boolean logic for the lookup tables (LUTs) are not included in this code, even though they would be needed in a production chip.)

Listing 5.3   Sample gate level HDL code

```
// ********************************************************
// ***** Multiplier for two unsigned 4-bit numbers *****
// ********************************************************

module UnsignedMultiply (
     clk,
     a,
     b,
     multiply_en,
     product);

input clk;
input [3:0] a;
input [3:0] b;
input multiply_en;
output [7:0] product;

wire clk ;
wire [3:0] a;
wire [3:0] b;
wire multiply_en ;
wire [7:0] product;
wire [3:0] count;
wire [7:0] product_c;
wire [3:0] a_c;
wire [7:0] product_10;
wire [3:0] b_c;
wire clk_c ;
wire count16 ;
wire un1_count_5_axb_1 ;
wire un1_count_5_axb_2 ;
wire un7_product_axb_1 ;
```

Listing 5.3   Sample gate level HDL code (Continued)

```
wire un7_product_axb_2 ;
wire un7_product_axb_3 ;
wire un7_product_axb_4 ;
wire un7_product_axb_5 ;
wire un1_un1_count16_i ;
wire multiply_en_c ;
wire un1_multiply_en_1_0 ;
wire product25_3_0_am ;
wire product25_3_0_bm ;
wire product25 ;
wire un7_product_axb_0 ;
wire un7_product_s_1 ;
wire un7_product_s_2 ;
wire un7_product_s_3 ;
wire un7_product_s_4 ;
wire un7_product_s_5 ;
wire un7_product_s_6 ;
wire un1_count_5_axb_0 ;
wire un1_count_5_axb_3 ;
wire un7_product_axb_6 ;
wire un1_count_5_s_1 ;
wire un1_count_5_s_2 ;
wire un1_count_5_s_3 ;
wire un7_product_cry_5 ;
wire un7_product_cry_4 ;
wire un7_product_cry_3 ;
wire un7_product_cry_2 ;
wire un7_product_cry_1 ;
wire un7_product_cry_0 ;
wire un1_count_5_cry_2 ;
wire un1_count_5_cry_1 ;
wire un1_count_5_cry_0 ;

LUT2_6 un1_count_5_axb_1_Z (
    .IO(count[1]),
```

Listing 5.3   Sample gate level HDL code (Continued)

```
        .I1(count16),
        .O(un1_count_5_axb_1));

LUT2_6 un1_count_5_axb_2_Z (
        .I0(count[2]),
        .I1(count16),
        .O(un1_count_5_axb_2));

LUT2_6 un7_product_axb_1_Z (
        .I0(product_c[1]),
        .I1(a_c[2]),
        .O(un7_product_axb_1));

LUT2_6 un7_product_axb_2_Z (
        .I0(product_c[2]),
        .I1(a_c[3]),
        .O(un7_product_axb_2));

LUT1_2 un7_product_axb_3_Z (
        .I0(product_c[3]),
        .O(un7_product_axb_3));

LUT1_2 un7_product_axb_4_Z (
        .I0(product_c[4]),
        .O(un7_product_axb_4));

LUT1_2 un7_product_axb_5_Z (
        .I0(product_c[5]),
        .O(un7_product_axb_5));

FDE \product_Z[7] (
        .Q(product_c[7]),
        .D(product_10[7]),
        .C(clk_c),
        .CE(un1_un1_count16_i));
```

Listing 5.3   Sample gate level HDL code (Continued)

```
FDE \product_Z[0] (
     .Q(product_c[0]),
     .D(product_10[0]),
     .C(clk_c),
     .CE(un1_un1_count16_i));

FDE \product_Z[1] (
     .Q(product_c[1]),
     .D(product_10[1]),
     .C(clk_c),
     .CE(un1_un1_count16_i));

FDE \product_Z[2] (
     .Q(product_c[2]),
     .D(product_10[2]),
     .C(clk_c),
     .CE(un1_un1_count16_i));

FDE \product_Z[3] (
     .Q(product_c[3]),
     .D(product_10[3]),
     .C(clk_c),
     .CE(un1_un1_count16_i));

FDE \product_Z[4] (
     .Q(product_c[4]),
     .D(product_10[4]),
     .C(clk_c),
     .CE(un1_un1_count16_i));

FDE \product_Z[5] (
     .Q(product_c[5]),
     .D(product_10[5]),
     .C(clk_c),
```

Listing 5.3   Sample gate level HDL code (Continued)

```
       .CE(un1_un1_count16_i));

FDE \product_Z[6]  (
      .Q(product_c[6]),
      .D(product_10[6]),
      .C(clk_c),
      .CE(un1_un1_count16_i));

LUT2_4 un1_multiply_en_1 (
      .I0(count16),
      .I1(multiply_en_c),
      .O(un1_multiply_en_1_0));

MUXF5 product25_3_0 (
      .I0(product25_3_0_am),
      .I1(product25_3_0_bm),
      .S(count[1]),
      .O(product25));

LUT3_D8 product25_3_0_bm_Z (
      .I0(count[0]),
      .I1(b_c[3]),
      .I2(b_c[2]),
      .O(product25_3_0_bm));

LUT3_D8 product25_3_0_am_Z (
      .I0(count[0]),
      .I1(b_c[1]),
      .I2(b_c[0]),
      .O(product25_3_0_am));

LUT4_A280 \product_10_Z[1]  (
      .I0(count16),
      .I1(product25),
      .I2(un7_product_axb_0),
```

Listing 5.3   Sample gate level HDL code (Continued)

```
    .I3(product_c[0]),
    .O(product_10[1]));

LUT4_A280 \product_10_Z[2]  (
    .I0(count16),
    .I1(product25),
    .I2(un7_product_s_1),
    .I3(product_c[1]),
    .O(product_10[2]));

LUT4_A280 \product_10_Z[3]  (
    .I0(count16),
    .I1(product25),
    .I2(un7_product_s_2),
    .I3(product_c[2]),
    .O(product_10[3]));

LUT4_A280 \product_10_Z[4]  (
    .I0(count16),
    .I1(product25),
    .I2(un7_product_s_3),
    .I3(product_c[3]),
    .O(product_10[4]));

LUT4_A280 \product_10_Z[5]  (
    .I0(count16),
    .I1(product25),
    .I2(un7_product_s_4),
    .I3(product_c[4]),
    .O(product_10[5]));

LUT4_A280 \product_10_Z[6]  (
    .I0(count16),
    .I1(product25),
    .I2(un7_product_s_5),
```

Listing 5.3   Sample gate level HDL code (Continued)

```
        .I3(product_c[5]),
        .O(product_10[6]));

LUT4_A280 \product_10_Z[7] (
        .I0(count16),
        .I1(product25),
        .I2(un7_product_s_6),
        .I3(product_c[6]),
        .O(product_10[7]));

LUT2_6 un1_count_5_axb_0_Z (
        .I0(count[0]),
        .I1(count16),
        .O(un1_count_5_axb_0));

LUT2_6 un1_count_5_axb_3_Z (
        .I0(count[3]),
        .I1(count16),
        .O(un1_count_5_axb_3));

LUT2_6 un7_product_axb_0_Z (
        .I0(product_c[0]),
        .I1(a_c[1]),
        .O(un7_product_axb_0));

LUT1_2 un7_product_axb_6_Z (
        .I0(product_c[6]),
        .O(un7_product_axb_6));

LUT4_FFFE count16_Z (
        .I0(count[2]),
        .I1(count[3]),
        .I2(count[0]),
        .I3(count[1]),
        .O(count16));
```

Listing 5.3   Sample gate level HDL code (Continued)

```
LUT3_80 \product_10_Z[0] (
        .I0(count16),
        .I1(product25),
        .I2(a_c[0]),
        .O(product_10[0]));

LUT2_E un1_un1_count16_i_Z (
        .I0(multiply_en_c),
        .I1(count16),
        .O(un1_un1_count16_i));

FDS \count_Z[0] (
        .Q(count[0]),
        .D(un1_count_5_axb_0),
        .C(clk_c),
        .S(un1_multiply_en_1_0));

FDS \count_Z[1] (
        .Q(count[1]),
        .D(un1_count_5_s_1),
        .C(clk_c),
        .S(un1_multiply_en_1_0));

FDS \count_Z[2] (
        .Q(count[2]),
        .D(un1_count_5_s_2),
        .C(clk_c),
        .S(un1_multiply_en_1_0));

FDS \count_Z[3] (
        .Q(count[3]),
        .D(un1_count_5_s_3),
        .C(clk_c),
        .S(un1_multiply_en_1_0));
```

Listing 5.3   Sample gate level HDL code (Continued)

```
XORCY un7_product_s_6_Z (
     .LI(un7_product_axb_6),
     .CI(un7_product_cry_5),
     .O(un7_product_s_6));

XORCY un7_product_s_5_Z (
     .LI(un7_product_axb_5),
     .CI(un7_product_cry_4),
     .O(un7_product_s_5));

MUXCY_L un7_product_cry_5_Z (
     .DI(GND),
     .CI(un7_product_cry_4),
     .S(un7_product_axb_5),
     .LO(un7_product_cry_5));

XORCY un7_product_s_4_Z (
     .LI(un7_product_axb_4),
     .CI(un7_product_cry_3),
     .O(un7_product_s_4));

MUXCY_L un7_product_cry_4_Z (
     .DI(GND),
     .CI(un7_product_cry_3),
     .S(un7_product_axb_4),
     .LO(un7_product_cry_4));

XORCY un7_product_s_3_Z (
     .LI(un7_product_axb_3),
     .CI(un7_product_cry_2),
     .O(un7_product_s_3));

MUXCY_L un7_product_cry_3_Z (
     .DI(GND),
```

Listing 5.3   Sample gate level HDL code (Continued)

```
        .CI(un7_product_cry_2),
        .S(un7_product_axb_3),
        .LO(un7_product_cry_3));

XORCY un7_product_s_2_Z (
        .LI(un7_product_axb_2),
        .CI(un7_product_cry_1),
        .O(un7_product_s_2));

MUXCY_L un7_product_cry_2_Z (
        .DI(product_c[2]),
        .CI(un7_product_cry_1),
        .S(un7_product_axb_2),
        .LO(un7_product_cry_2));

XORCY un7_product_s_1_Z (
        .LI(un7_product_axb_1),
        .CI(un7_product_cry_0),
        .O(un7_product_s_1));

MUXCY_L un7_product_cry_1_Z (
        .DI(product_c[1]),
        .CI(un7_product_cry_0),
        .S(un7_product_axb_1),
        .LO(un7_product_cry_1));

MUXCY_L un7_product_cry_0_Z (
        .DI(product_c[0]),
        .CI(GND),
        .S(un7_product_axb_0),
        .LO(un7_product_cry_0));

XORCY un1_count_5_s_3_Z (
        .LI(un1_count_5_axb_3),
        .CI(un1_count_5_cry_2),
```

Listing 5.3   Sample gate level HDL code (Continued)

```
        .O(un1_count_5_s_3));

XORCY un1_count_5_s_2_Z (
        .LI(un1_count_5_axb_2),
        .CI(un1_count_5_cry_1),
        .O(un1_count_5_s_2));

MUXCY_L un1_count_5_cry_2_Z (
        .DI(count[2]),
        .CI(un1_count_5_cry_1),
        .S(un1_count_5_axb_2),
        .LO(un1_count_5_cry_2));

XORCY un1_count_5_s_1_Z (
        .LI(un1_count_5_axb_1),
        .CI(un1_count_5_cry_0),
        .O(un1_count_5_s_1));

MUXCY_L un1_count_5_cry_1_Z (
        .DI(count[1]),
        .CI(un1_count_5_cry_0),
        .S(un1_count_5_axb_1),
        .LO(un1_count_5_cry_1));

MUXCY_L un1_count_5_cry_0_Z (
        .DI(count[0]),
        .CI(GND),
        .S(un1_count_5_axb_0),
        .LO(un1_count_5_cry_0));
endmodule /* UnsignedMultiply */
```

Finally, the lowest level is that of a switch level model. A switch level model specifies the actual transistor switches that are combined to make gates. Digital design is never done at this level. Switch level code can be used for physical design of an ASIC and can also be used for the design of analog devices.

The advantage of HDLs is that they enable all of these different levels of modeling within the same language. This makes all the stages of design very convenient to implement. You don't need to learn different tools. You can easily simulate the design at a behavioral level, and then substitute various behavioral code modules with structural code modules. For system simulation, this allows you to analyze your entire project using the same set of tools. First, you can test and optimize the algorithms. Next, you can use the behavioral models to partition the hardware into boards, ASIC, and FPGAs. You can then write the RTL code and substitute it for behavioral blocks, one at a time, to easily test the functionality of each block. From that, you can synthesize the design, creating gate and switch level blocks that can be resimulated with timing numbers to get actual performance measurements. Finally, you can use this low-level code to generate a netlist for layout. All stages of the design have been performed using the same basic tool.

The main HDLs in existence today are Verilog and VHDL. Both are open standards, maintained by standards groups of the Institute of Electrical and Electronic Engineers (IEEE). VHDL is maintained as IEEE-STD-1076; Verilog is maintained as IEEE-STD-1364. Although some engineers prefer one language over the other, the differences are minor. As these standard languages progress with new versions, the differences become even fewer. Also, several languages, including C++, are being offered as a system level language, which would enable engineers to design and simulate an entire system consisting of multiple chips, boards, and software. These system level design languages are still evolving.

5.2 Top-Down Design

Top-down design is the design methodology whereby high level functions are defined first, and the lower level implementation details are filled in later. A design can be viewed as a hierarchical tree, as shown in Figure 5.1. The top level block represents the entire chip. The next lower level blocks also represent the entire chip but divided into the major function blocks of the chip. Intermediate level blocks divide the functionality into more manageable pieces. The bottom level contains only gates and macrofunctions, which are vendor-supplied high level functions.

5.2.1   Use of Hardware Design Languages

Top-down design methodology lends itself particularly well to using HDLs, the generally accepted method of designing complex CPLDs and FPGAs. Each block in the design corresponds to the code for a self-contained module. The top-level blocks correspond to the behavioral models that comprise the chip. The intermediate levels correspond to the RTL models that will become input to the synthesis process. The lowest level of the hierarchy corresponds to gate level code

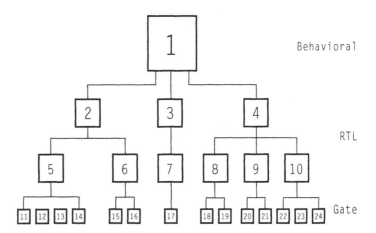

Figure 5.1   Top-down design

which is output from the synthesis software and which directly represents logic structures within the chip.

5.2.2   Written Specifications

Top-down design methodology works hand in hand with a written specification that, as discussed in Chapter 4, is an essential starting point for any design. The specification must include general aspects of the design, including the major functional blocks. The highest blocks of a top-down design are behavioral level models that correspond to the major functional blocks described in the specification. Thus, using a top-down design approach, the specification becomes a starting point for the actual HDL code. Specification changes can immediately be turned into HDL design changes, and design changes can be quickly and easily translated back to the specification, keeping the specification accurate and up to date.

5.2.3   Allocating Resources

These days, chips typically incorporate a large number of gates and a very high level of functionality. A top-down approach simplifies the design task and allows more than one engineer, when necessary, to design the chip. For example, the lead designer or the system architect may be responsible for the specification and the top-level block. Engineers in the design team may each be responsible for one or several intermediate blocks, depending on their strengths, experience, and abilities. An experienced ALU designer may be responsible for the ALU block and several other blocks. A junior engineer can work on a smaller block, such as a bus controller. Each engineer can work in parallel, writing code and simulating, until it is time to integrate the pieces into a single design. No one person can slow down the entire design. With a top-down design, your not-too-bright colleague in the next cubicle won't delay the entire project or make you look bad. That may be the single best reason for using this design methodology.

5.2.4   Design Partitioning

Even if you are the only engineer designing the chip, this methodology allows you to break the design into simpler functions that you (or others) can design and simulate independently from the rest of the design. A large, complex design becomes a series of independent smaller ones that are easier to design and simulate.

5.2.5   Flexibility and Optimization

Top-down design allows flexibility. Teams can remove sections of the design and replace them with higher-performance or optimized designs without affecting other sections of the design. Adding new or improved functionality involves simply redesigning one section of the design and substituting it for the current section.

5.2.6   Reusability

Reusability is an important topic in chip design these days. In the days when a CPLD consisted of a few small state machines, it was no big deal to design it from scratch. Nowadays, CPLDs and FPGAs contain so much logic that reusing any function from a previous design can save days, weeks, or months of design time. When one group has already designed a certain function, say a fast, efficient 64-bit multiplier, HDLs allow you to take the design and reuse it in your design. If you need a 64-bit multiplier, you can simply take the designed, verified code and plop it into your design. Or you can purchase the code from a third party. But it will only fit easily into your design if you have used a top-down approach to break the design into smaller pieces, one of which is a 64-bit multiplier.

5.2.7   Floorplanning

Floorplanning is another important topic in chip design these days. As chips become larger, it may be necessary to help the design tools place the various functions in the device. If you have used a top-down approach, you will be able to plan the placement of each block in the chip. The FBs or CLBs that implement the logic in each block can be placed in proximity to each other. The relationship between blocks will also be apparent, and so you can understand which blocks should be placed near each other.

5.2.8 Verification

Verification, discussed at length in Chapter 6, has become an extremely important aspect of the design process, but can be very resource-intensive and thus often needs to be optimized. Top-down design is one important means for improving verification. A top-down design approach allows each module to be simulated independently from the rest of the design. This is important for complex designs where an entire design can take weeks to simulate and days to debug. By using a top-down approach, design teams can efficiently perform behavioral, RTL, and gate level simulations and use the results to verify functionality at each level of design.

In summary, top-down design facilitates these good design practices:

- Use of hardware design languages
- Writing accurate and up-to-date specifications
- Allocation of resources for the design task
- Simplification and easy partitioning of the design task
- Flexibility in experimenting with different designs and optimizing the design
- Reusing previous designs
- Floorplanning
- Improved verification and less time spent on verification

5.2.9 Know the Architecture

Look at the particular architecture for the CPLD or FPGA that you are using to determine which logic devices fit best into it. You should choose a device with an architecture that fits well with your particular design. In addition, as you design, keep in mind the architecture of the device. For example, you may be using a CPLD that includes exclusive ORs. When you are deciding which kind of error detection to use, you could perform parity checking efficiently in this device. Similarly, if the device includes a fast carry chain, make sure that you are able to use it for any adders that you are designing.

Many FPGA and CPLD vendors now include specialized logic functions in their devices. For example, vendors may offer a device with a built-in digital signal processor (DSP). This device will not be useful, and is the wrong choice, if your design does not use a DSP. On the other hand, if you are implementing signal processing functions, you should make sure you use this DSP function as much as possible throughout the design.

The vendor will be able to offer advice about their device architecture and how to efficiently utilize it. Most synthesis tools can target their results to a specific FPGA or CPLD family from a specific vendor, taking advantage of the architecture to provide you with faster, more optimal designs.

5.3 Synchronous Design

One of the most important concepts in chip design, and one of the hardest to enforce on novice chip designers, is that of synchronous design. Once a chip designer uncovers a problem due to a design that is not synchronous (i.e., asynchronous) and attempts to fix it, he or she usually becomes an evangelical convert to synchronous design practices. This is because asynchronous design problems often appear intermittently due to subtle variations in the voltage, temperature, or semiconductor process. Or they may appear only when the vendor changes its semiconductor process. Asynchronous designs that work for years in one process may suddenly fail when the programmable part is manufactured using a newer process.

Unlike technologies like printed circuit boards, the semiconductor processes for creating FPGAs change very rapidly. Moore's Law, an observation about semiconductor technology improvements, currently says that the number of transistors per square inch doubles every 18 months. This doubling is due to rapid increases in semiconductor process technology and advances in the machinery used to create silicon structures. Due to these improvements, the FPGA or CPLD device that holds your design today will have different, faster timing parameters than the one that holds your design a year from now. The vendor will no doubt have improved its process by that time.

Even if you were certain that the semiconductor process for your programmable device would remain constant for each device in your system, each process has natural variations from chip to chip and even within a single chip. To add even more uncertainty, the exact timing for a programmable device depends on the specific routing and logic implementation. Essentially, you cannot determine exact delay numbers; you can only know timing ranges and relative delays. Synchronous design is a formal methodology for ensuring that your design will work correctly and within your speed requirements as long as the timing numbers remain within certain ranges and with delays that remain relatively controlled, if not absolutely controlled.

Synchronous design is not only more reliable than asynchronous design, but for the most part, EDA tools now assume that your design is synchronous. In the early days of EDA software for digital circuits, the tools made no assumptions about the design. As chip designs grew, the software tools became more difficult to develop, the algorithms became more complex, and the tools became slower and less efficient. The EDA vendors finally realized that synchronous design was required anyway, for the reasons I gave previously. So the EDA vendors also began enforcing synchronous design rules, which made their algorithms simpler, the software complexity more manageable, and the tools faster and more efficient.

5.3.1   Five Rules of Synchronous Design

I use five rules to define synchronous design for a single clock domain. (A single clock domain means that all logic is clocked by a single clock signal.)

1. All data is passed through combinatorial logic, and through delay elements, typically flip-flops, that are synchronized to a single clock.

2. Delay is always controlled by delay elements, not combinatorial logic.

3. No signal that is generated by combinatorial logic can be fed back to the same combinatorial logic without first going through a synchronizing delay element.

4. Clocks cannot be gated; clocks must go directly to the clock inputs of the delay elements without going through any combinatorial logic.

5. Data signals must go only to combinatorial logic or data inputs of delay elements.

Note that I use the term "delay elements." Typically, these elements will be flip-flops because those are the common delay element devices in use. Strictly speaking, the delay elements do not need to be flip-flops, they can be any element whose delay is predictable and synchronized to a clock signal.

A design may have multiple clocks and thus multiple clock domains. In other words, there will be logic clocked by one clock signal and logic clocked by another clock signal, but the design must treat all signals passed between the two domains as asynchronous signals. In Section Section 5.3.7, you will see how to deal with asynchronous signals.

The following sections cover common asynchronous design problems, what specific problems they can cause, and how to design the same functionality using synchronous logic. In my career, I have seen many of these problems in real designs and, unfortunately, I have had to debug many of them.

5.3.2   Race Conditions

Figure 5.2 shows an asynchronous race condition where a clock signal is connected to the asynchronous reset of a flip-flop. This violates rules 2 and either 4 or 5. It violates rule 2 because an asynchronous reset has a delay that is controlled by the internal design of the flip-flop, not by a delay element. It violates rule 4 if SIG2 is a clock signal, because it should not go to the CLR input. Otherwise, if SIG2 is a data signal, it should not go to the CLK input.

Gate Count Controversy

What, exactly is a gate count? The term comes from ASIC designs, specifically gate array ASICs, where designs are eventually reduced to the simplest elements consisting of logic gates — NANDs, NORs, buffers, and inverters. When FPGA vendors were courting ASIC designers, it made sense for them to compare the amount of logic that could be put into an FPGA with the amount that could be put into an ASIC. Because ASIC designers used gate counts, FPGA vendors started advertising gate counts for their devices.

The FPGA gate count had two problems. First, FPGAs don't have gates. They have larger grain logic such as flip-flops, and lookup tables that designers can use to implement Boolean equations that don't depend on gates. For example, the equation

A = B & C & D & E & F

requires one 5-input AND gate in an ASIC or one 5-LUT in an FPGA. However, the equation

A = ((B & C) | (D & E)) & ~F

requires five gates — three AND gates, one OR gate, and an inverter — in an ASIC, but still only one 5-LUT in an FPGA. So a gate count isn't an accurate measure of the logic a designer can fit into an FPGA.

The second problem is that utilization of the available logic in an FPGA is not nearly 100 percent and is very application dependant. Utilization percentages of 60 to 80 are much more common for any given

How does this logic behave? When SIG2 is low, the flip-flop is reset to a low state. On the rising edge of SIG2, the designer wants the output, OUT, to change to reflect the current state of the input, SIG1. Unfortunately, because we do not know the exact internal timing of the flip-flop or the routing delay of the signal to the clock versus the routing delay of the reset input, we cannot know which signal will effectively arrive at the appropriate logic first — the clock or the reset. This is a race condition. If the clock rising edge arrives first, the output will remain low. If the reset signal arrives first, the output will go high. A slight change in temperature, voltage, or pro-

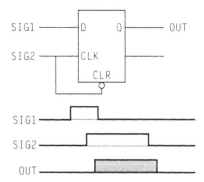

Figure 5.2 Asynchronous: Race condition. Note that OUT goes to an undefined state.

design. So although an FPGA may be able to hold the equivalent of a 1 million–gate design, in theory, it is unlikely that a designer can actually fit and successfully route any particular 1 million–gate design in such a FPGA.

For this reason, the different FPGA vendors attacked their competitors' gate count numbers. Then, years ago, a non-profit organization called PREP created what was called the PREP benchmarks. These benchmarks consisted of standard designs to be synthesized, placed, and routed into FPGAs from different vendors. The idea was that this would be a standard way of comparing the densities, routability, power consumption, and speed of these different FPGAs. This seemed like a better solution than the simple gate count. The different vendors, however, fought vehemently and many refused to participate in the benchmarks, claiming that some of the benchmark designs conformed to their competitors' architectures, producing deceptively better results. They also claimed that some synthesis and place and route tools used for benchmarking did a better job of optimizing their competitors' FPGAs, again making their competitors look better on these specific designs. Their arguments were not without merit and PREP eventually disbanded.

For some reason, though, gate count has come to be an accepted standard among FPGA vendors. They no longer complain, publicly at least, that their competitors are using misleading methods of counting available gates in their FPGAs. As a user of the FPGAs, however, you should understand that gate counts are a very rough estimate of capacity. Use them only for making rough determinations and rough comparisons.

cess may cause a chip that works correctly to suddenly work incorrectly because the order of arrival of the two signals changes.

My first step when creating a synchronous design, or converting an asynchronous design to a synchronous one, is to draw a state diagram. Although this may seem like overkill for such a small function, I find it useful to organize my thoughts and make sure that I've covered all of the possible conditions. The state diagram for this function is shown in Figure 5.3. From this diagram, it is easy to design the more reliable, synchronous solution shown in Figure 5.4. Here the flip-flop is reset synchronously on the rising edge of a fast clock. I've introduced a new signal, STATE, that together with the OUT signal,

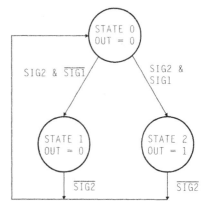

Figure 5.3   Synchronous state diagram

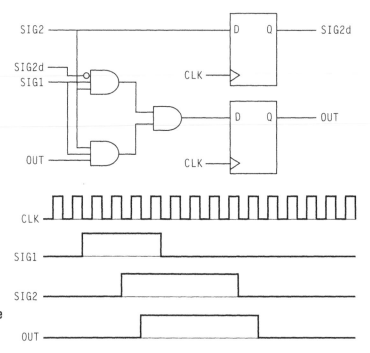

Figure 5.4 Synchronous: No race condition

will uniquely identify the three states of the FSM. This circuit performs the correct function, and as long as SIG1 and SIG2 are produced synchronously — they change only after the rising edge of CLK — there is no race condition.

Now some people may argue that the synchronous design uses more logic, adding delay and using up expensive die space. They may also argue that the fast clock means that this design will consume more power. (This is especially true if it is implemented in CMOS, because CMOS devices consume power only while there is a logic transition. In this design, the flip-flops will consume power on every clock edge.) Finally, these people may argue that this design introduces extra signals that require more routing resources, add delay, and again, that consume precious die space. All of this is true. This design, however, will work reliably, and the previous design will not. End of argument.

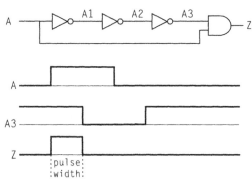

Figure 5.5 Asynchronous: Delay dependent logic

5.3.3 Delay Dependent Logic

Figure 5.5 shows an asynchronous circuit used to create a pulse. The pulse width depends very explicitly on the delay of the individual logic gates. If the semiconductor process used to manufacture the chip should change, making the delay shorter, the pulse width will shorten also, to the point where the logic that it feeds may not recognize it at all. Because chip vendors are continually speeding up their processes, you can be certain that this type of design will eventually fail for some new batch of chips.

A synchronous version of a pulse generator is shown in Figure 5.6. This pulse depends only on the clock period. As our rule number

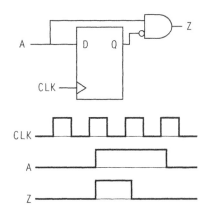

Figure 5.6 Synchronous: Delay independent logic

2 of synchronous design states, delay must always be controlled by delay elements. Changes to the semiconductor process will not cause any significant change in the pulse width for this design.

5.3.4 Hold Time Violations

Figure 5.7 shows an asynchronous circuit with a hold time violation. Hold time violations occur when data changes around the same time as the clock edge; it is uncertain which value will be registered by the clock — the value of the data input right before the clock edge or the value right after the clock edge. It all depends on the internal characteristics of the flip-flop. This can also result in a metastability problem, as discussed later.

The circuit in Figure 5.8 fixes this problem by putting both flip-flops on the same clock and using a flip-flop with an enable input. A pulse generator creates a pulse, signal Dp3, by ANDing signal D3 and a signal D3d, which is D3 delayed by a single clock cycle. The pulse D3p enables the flip-flop for one clock cycle.

The pulse generator also turns out to be very useful for synchronous design, when you want to clock data into a flip-flop after a particular event.

5.3.5 Glitches

A glitch can occur due to small delays in a circuit, such as that shown in Figure 5.9. This particular example is one I like because the problem is not obvious at first. Here, a multiplexer switches between selecting two high inputs. It would appear, as it did to me when I was first shown this example, that the output

Changing Processes

Years ago I was working on a project designing some controller boards for a small client company. The vice president of manufacturing approached me and told me about a problem they were having and asked if I had any ideas. It seems that they had been shipping a particular board for about two years. Suddenly, every board would fail the preship tests they ran on it. They had assigned an engineer to look into it, but he couldn't find anything. What was particularly strange was that no part of the design had changed in two years.

I took time to look at the board and at the tests they were running on it. I narrowed the problem down to a particular FPGA and began examining the design. I found that there was one asynchronous circuit where a logic signal was being used to clock a flip-flop. I decided to call up the FPGA vendor and ask them whether they had recently changed their manufacturing process. They said that they had moved their devices over to a faster semiconductor process about two months ago. That corresponded exactly to the time when these boards started failing.

This illustrates a very important point about synchronous design. When you design synchronously, you are immune to process speedups because the chip vendor ensures that any speedups result with clock signals that are still much faster than data signals. However, if you have designed an asynchronous circuit, it works because the relationship between data signals has a specific timing relationship. In a new semiconductor process, these relationships between data signals may no longer hold.

Also, you will notice that FPGA vendors do not specify minimum delay times. This is because they want to have the ability to move older devices to newer, faster processes. When a semiconductor process is new, the bugs haven't been worked out, and the yields tend to be low. The vendor will charge more for denser, faster chips based on this process. Once the bugs are worked out and yields go up to a reasonable level, the vendor does not want to maintain two different processes because it is too expensive. Instead, the vendor will move the "slower" chips over to the faster process. So these so-called "slower" chips are now faster than before. As long as they have not specified the minimum times, the timing numbers for these "slower" chips are still within the specifications. And as long as you have designed synchronously, you will not have the problem that this client of mine did.

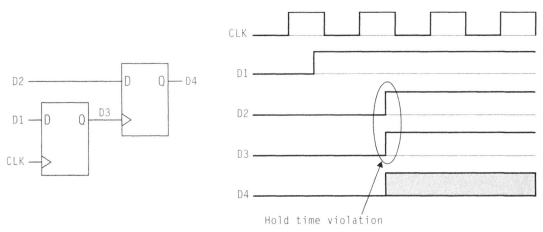

Figure 5.7   Asynchronous: Hold time violation

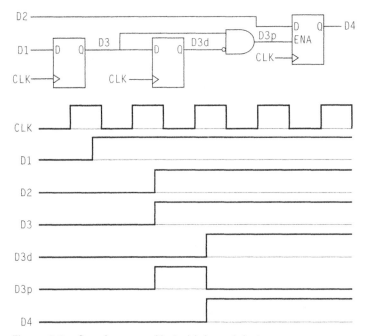

Figure 5.8   Synchronous: No hold time violation

would be high no matter what the value of the select input. One should be able to change the select input from low to high and back to low again and still get a high value out. In practice, though, the multiplexer produces a glitch when switching the select input. This is because of the internal design of the multiplexer, as shown in Figure 5.9. Due to the delay of the inverter on the select

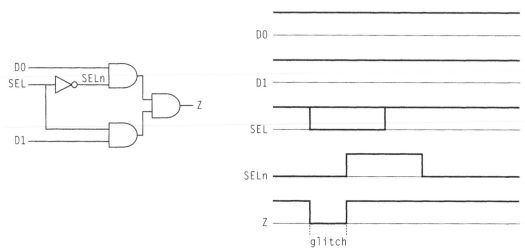

Figure 5.9   Asynchronous: Glitch

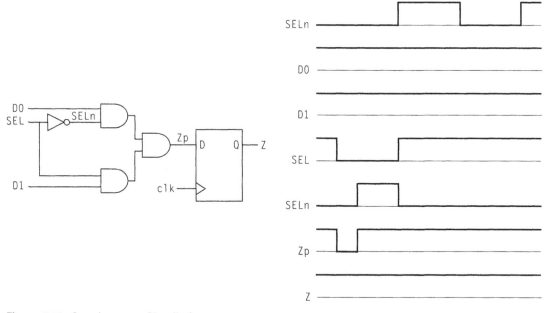

Figure 5.10 Synchronous: No glitch

input, there is a short time when signals SEL and SELn are both low. Thus nei-ther input is selected, causing the output to go low.

Synchronizing this output by sending it through a flip-flop, as shown in Fig-ure 5.10, ensures that this glitch will not appear on the output and will not affect logic further downstream. As long as the timing calculations have been performed correctly, the entire design is synchronous, and the device is operated below the maximum clock frequency for the design, glitches such as this one will settle before the next clock edge.

5.3.6 Gated Clocking

Figure 5.11 shows an example of gated clocking. This violates the fourth and fifth rules of synchronous design because the circuit has data signals going to clock inputs and clock signals going to data inputs. This kind of clock gating will produce problems that will be particularly bad in FPGAs, because the GATE signal can easily be delayed so that the clock signal rises before the GATE signal can prevent it. Data then gets clocked into the flip-flop on a cycle when it is not supposed to.

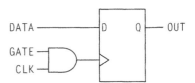

Figure 5.11 Asynchronous: Clock gating

The correct way to enable and disable outputs is not by putting logic on the clock input, but by putting logic on the data input, as shown in Figure 5.12. Essentially, this circuit consists of an enable flip-flop that has a data signal, GATE, which enables and disables the flip-flop. In this synchronous design, the flip-flop is always being clocked directly by the CLK signal. The GATE input controls the mux on the input, to determine whether the new data gets clocked in or the old data gets clocked back in.

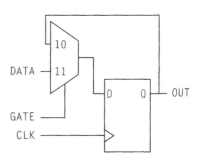

Figure 5.12 Synchronous: Logic gating

5.3.7 Asynchronous Signals and Metastability

One of the great buzzwords, and often-misunderstood concepts, of synchronous design is metastability. I have found that even engineers who believe they understand the issue, may not be completely aware of all of the issues. I know that I had a good knowledge of metastability before I began writing about it. When I write about a topic, though, I make sure I understand it exactly. After doing some research on metastability, I realized that I still hadn't completely appreciated some issues.

Metastability refers to a condition that arises when an asynchronous signal is clocked into a synchronous flip-flop. The term can be easily understood from its equivalent in basic physics. Figure 5.14 shows a rigid pendulum in two possible

The Enable Flip-Flop

The enable flip-flop is an important piece of logic for synchronous design. Many pieces of asynchronous logic can be turned into synchronous logic with the use of an enable flip-flop. The enable flip-flop allows data to be selectively clocked into a flip-flop rather than being clocked in on every clock edge.

The logic for an enable flip-flop is simple, as shown in Figure 5.13. It consists of a mux placed in the data path going to a normal flip-flop. When the enable signal is asserted, the data goes through the

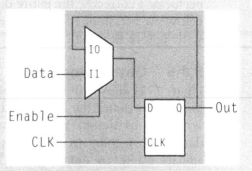

Figure 5.13 An enable flip-flop

mux and is clocked into the D-input at the next clock edge. When the enable signal is not asserted, the output of the flip-flop is simply fed back, through the mux, into the data input of the flip-flop so that the data is continually clocked in on each clock edge.

stable states. In the first, the pendulum is hanging down. This is a stable state. The pendulum will tend to go into this state. If you tweak the pendulum, it will swing back and forth for a while and eventually end up back where it started.

The second part of the figure shows a rigid pendulum in a metastable state. If the pendulum is exactly in this state, upside-down, it will remain in this state indefinitely. However, if some small perturbation occurs — you tweak the pendulum in this state — the pendulum will swing down and eventually settle into the first, stable state. In other words, a metastable state is a precarious one in which an object will not remain for very long.

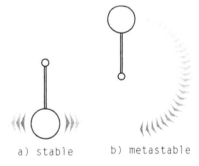

Figure 5.14 Stable states of a rigid pendulum

Although chip designers would prefer a completely synchronous world, the unfortunate fact is that signals coming into a chip will depend on a user pushing a button or an interrupt from a processor, or will be generated by a clock that is different from the one used by the chip. In these cases, designers must synchronize the asynchronous signal to the chip clock so that it can be used by the internal circuitry. The designer must do this carefully in order to avoid metastability problems. Figure 5.15 shows a circuit with

Clock Gating At Processor Companies

In this section, I have railed against the process of gating clocks. Gated clocks constitute asynchronous design, which will not produce a reliable design. To confuse you a little, I will add, if you do not know already, that clock gating is an accepted means of turning off functionality in large designs, specifically microprocessors. Most chip designs are implemented in CMOS; CMOS devices draw significant power while they are switching. So any CMOS device will use power while it is being clocked. In order to reduce power consumption, particularly in chips designed for low power systems such as laptops, entire functional blocks have their clocks gated off when not in use.

So why is it that the large microprocessor manufacturers can use a technique that I am telling you not to use? Essentially they have a luxury that you do not have. First, the design teams at these companies have access to detailed circuit level simulations that can determine the timing more accurately than you can. These design teams work closely with the process engineers and the layout designers to calculate very exact timing numbers in order to avoid race conditions or other hazards due to asynchronous design.

Second, when the process engineers speed up a semiconductor process, changing the timing specifications, you can be sure that the design engineers know about it ahead of time. This gives them enough time to recalculate all of the critical timing and change the design and/or the layout to compensate for the new process.

On the other hand, when CPLD and FPGA vendors plan to change their process, it is unlikely that they will notify you beforehand. And if they did, would you really want to spend engineering time and resources redesigning your chip each time they change their processes? Definitely not. For this reason, the microprocessor manufacturers can gate their clocks in order to reduce power but you, unfortunately, should not.

potential metastability. If the ASYNC_IN signal goes high around the same time as the clock, it creates an unavoidable hold time violation. Flip-flop FF1 can go into a metastable state. If certain internal transistors do not have enough time to fully charge to the correct level, the output of flip-flop FF1, signal IN, can actually go to an undefined voltage level, somewhere between a logic 0 and logic 1. This "metalevel" will remain until the transistor voltage leaks off, or "decays," or until the next clock cycle when a good clean value gets clocked in. In some cases, depending on the internal structure of the flip-flop, the metalevel may be a signal that oscillates between a good 0 value and a good 1 value.

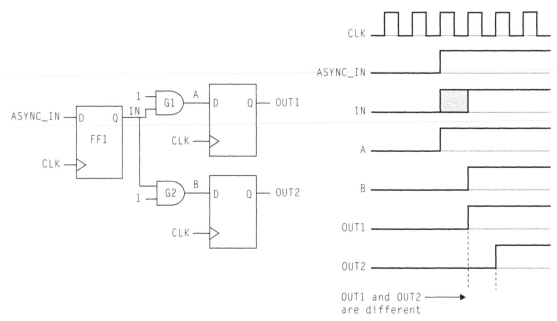

Figure 5.15 Metastability — the problem

This is where many engineers stop. This metalevel voltage on signal IN, though, is not really the problem. During the clock cycle, the gates driven by signal IN may interpret this metalevel differently. In the figure, the upper AND gate, G1, sees the level as a logic 1, whereas the lower AND gate, G2, sees it as a logic 0. This could occur because the two gates have different input thresholds because of process variations or power voltage variations throughout the die. It is possible that one gate is near the output of FF1, and the other is far away. Such differences in routing can cause the signal to change enough at the input to each gate to be interpreted differently.

In normal operation, OUT1 and OUT2 should always be the same value. Instead, we have created a condition that cannot occur according to the rules of logic. This condition is completely unpredictable. This is the problem with metastability — not that an output has a bad voltage, but that a single signal is interpreted differently by different pieces of logic. This problem will send the logic into an unexpected, unpredictable state from which it may never return. Metastability can permanently lock up your chip.

The "solution" to this metastability problem is shown in Figure 5.16. By placing a synchronizer flip-flop, S1, in front of the logic, the synchronized input, SYNC_IN, will be sampled by only one device, flip-flop FF1, and be interpreted only as a logic 0 or 1. The output of flip-flop FF1, IN, will be either a clean 1 or a clean 0 signal. The upper and lower gates, G1 and G2, will both sample the same logic level on signal IN.

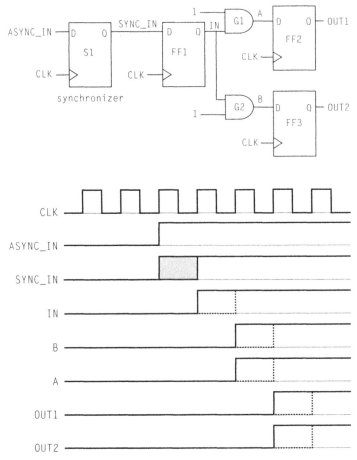

Figure 5.16 Metastability — the "solution"

There is still a very small but nonzero probability that a metastable signal SYNC_IN, will cause the output of flip-flop FF1, signal IN, to go metastable on the next clock edge, creating the same problem as before. Why would signal IN go metastable? A metalevel voltage on the input may cause a capacitor in flip-flop FF1 to change part way, creating a metalevel output. Of course, there is still an advantage with the synchronizer flip-flop. Because a device does not prefer to remain in a metastable state, there is a good chance that it has decayed into a stable state by the next clock edge. So this creates a time period — one clock period — during which the metastable device can stabilize before a problem occurs.

It seems that in either case, the metastability problem is solved. Or is it? I have put the word "solution" in quotation marks for a very good reason. Because this problem involves a probabilistic event, there is a possibility that the signal SYNC_IN will not decay to a valid logic level within one clock period. In this case, the next flip-flop will sample a metalevel value, and there is again a possibility that the output of flip-flop FF1, signal IN, will be indeterminate. At higher frequencies, this possibility increases.

Unfortunately, there is no certain solution to this problem. Some vendors provide special synchronizer flip-flops whose output transistors decay very quickly. Also, inserting more synchronizer flip-flops reduces the probability of metastability, but doings so will never reduce the probability to zero. The correct action involves discussing metastability problems with the vendor, and including enough synchronizing flip-flops to reduce the probability so that the problem is unlikely to occur within the lifetime of the product.

A good way to judge a CPLD or FPGA vendor is to ask them for metastability data and solutions. A good vendor will have run tests on their flip-flops and have characterized the probability of creating a metastable state. They may have special synchronizing flip-flops and they should have rules for the number of flip-flops needed at a given clock frequency, to reduce the odds of a problem due to metastability to a reasonable number.

5.3.8 Allowable Uses of Asynchronous Logic

Now that I've gone through a long argument against asynchronous design, I will tell you the few exceptions that I have found to this rule. I used to say that there were no exceptions. But experience always shows that every rule has an exception (except that rule). However, approach these exceptions with extreme caution and consideration.

Asynchronous Reset

Sometimes it is acceptable, or even preferable, to use an asynchronous reset throughout a design. If the vendor's library includes flip-flops with asynchronous reset inputs, designers can tie the reset input to a master reset in order to reduce the routing congestion and to reduce the logic required for a synchronous reset. FPGAs and CPLDs have master reset signals built into the architecture. Using these signals to reset state machines frees up interconnect for other uses. Because routing resources are often the limiting factor in the density of an FPGA design, you should take advantage of the asynchronous reset input to the flip-flops.

The rules to follow for an asynchronous reset are:

- Use it only to initialize the chip. Asynchronous resets should not occur during normal operation.

Synchronizer Delay

Notice that each synchronizer flip-flop will delay the input signal by one clock cycle before it is recognized by the internal circuitry of the chip. This may at first seem to be a problem, but it is not. Given that the external signal is asynchronous, by definition the exact time that it is asserted will not be deterministic. You may need to respond to it within a set time period, but that time period should be orders of magnitude greater than several clock cycles. If this delay is a problem in your design, most likely this input should not be an asynchronous signal. Instead, you should generate this signal by logic that uses the same clock that is used in the rest of the chip, which will eliminate the metastability problem altogether.

- Assert the reset signal for at least one clock cycle.

- After reset, ensure that the chip is in a stable state such that no flip-flops will change until an input changes. In other words, after reset every state machine should be in an idle state waiting for an input signal to change.

- The inputs to the chip should be stable and not change for at least one clock cycle after the reset is removed.

Asynchronous Latches on Inputs

Some buses, such as the VME bus, are designed to be asynchronous. In order to interface with these buses, designers need to use asynchronous latches to capture addresses or data. Once the data is captured, it must be synchronized to the internal clock. One suitable technique is to synchronize each incoming signal with its own synchronizing flip-flop. (This is what I suggested in the previous discussion on metastability.)

However, it is usually much more efficient to use asynchronous latches to capture the bus signals initially. Many buses have an address latch enable (ALE)

Synchronous VME Bus Is Not Synchronous

The VME bus has been in existence for a relatively long time now. It's a standard, a workhorse. In use since the early days of microprocessors, it's the granddaddy of all buses. And it's asynchronous, like most of the buses that came after it. Asynchronous buses are easier to implement over different media using various components. Synchronous buses require a lot of coordination between different devices, and they need carefully controlled timing.

When synchronous design became more recognized and more important for chip design for all of the reasons I discussed, synchronous buses such as PCI and SBUS started popping up. Synchronous buses have tighter timing requirements, but they can be much more efficient at transferring data. Some engineer or standards committee or perhaps a marketing person decided to make a synchronous VME bus by adding a clock to it. Unfortunately, no relationship exists between the signals of the bus and the clock. The clock was simply added to the existing asynchronous bus, resulting in an asynchronous bus with a clock.

I discovered this the hard way when I was asked to interface an FPGA with the "synchronous" VME bus. The overhead of logic and clock cycles required to synchronize this "synchronous" bus made data transfers very inefficient. My advice is this: When interfacing to a bus, look at the timing relationships to determine whether it is really synchronous. If these relationships are synchronous, a synchronous interface will be very efficient. Otherwise, despite the label that the bus may have, treat it as asynchronous and design the interface accordingly.

signal to latch addresses and a data strobe (DSTROBE) to latch data. Unless your chip uses a clock that has a frequency much higher than that of the bus, attempting to synchronize all of these signals will cause a large amount of overhead and may actually create timing problems rather than eliminate them. Instead, you can latch the inputs asynchronously and then synchronize the signal that gets asserted last in the protocol, usually the data strobe, to the internal clock. By the time this late signal has been synchronized, you can be certain that all of the inputs are stable.

5.4 Floating Nodes

Floating nodes are internal nodes of a circuit that are not driven to a logic 0 or logic 1. They should always be avoided. An example of a potential floating node is shown in Figure 5.17. If signals SEL_A and SEL_B are both not asserted, signal OUT will float to an unknown level. Downstream logic may interpret OUT as a logic 1 or a logic 0, or the floating signal may create a metastable state. In particular, any CMOS circuitry that uses signal OUT as an input will use up power because CMOS dissipates power when the input is in the threshold region. The signal OUT will typically float somewhere in the threshold region. Also, even if downstream logic is not using this signal, the signal can bounce up and down, causing noise in the system and inducing noise in surrounding signals.

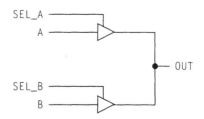

Figure 5.17 Floating nodes —
the problem
NOTE: SEL_A and SEL_B
are mutually exclusive

Two solutions to the floating node problem are shown in Figure 5.18. At the top, signal OUT is pulled up using an internal pull-up resistor. This simple fix ensures that when both select signals are not asserted, OUT will be pulled to a good logic level. Note that the pull up represented in the picture may be a passive resistor, or it may be an active pull up circuit that can be faster and more power conservative.

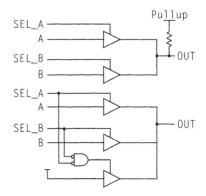

Figure 5.18 Floating nodes —
solutions
NOTE: SEL_A and SEL_B
are mutually exclusive

The other solution, shown at the bottom of the figure, is to make sure that something is driving the output at all times. A third select signal is created that drives the OUT signal to a good level when neither of the other normal select signals are asserted.

5.5 Bus Contention

Bus contention occurs when two outputs drive the same signal at the same time, as shown in Figure 5.20. This reduces the reliability of the chip because it has multiple drivers fighting each other to drive a common output. If bus contention occurs regularly, even for short times, the possibility of damage to the drivers increases.

One place where this can occur, and that is often ignored, is during the turn-around of a bus. In a synchronous bus, when one device is driving the bus during one clock cycle and a different device is driving during the next clock cycle, there is a short time when both devices may be driving the bus, as shown in Figure 5.19.

To avoid contention problems, the designer must ensure that both drivers cannot be asserted simultaneously. This can be accomplished by inserting additional logic, as shown in Figure 5.21. The logic for each buffer enable has been modified so that a buffer is not turned on until its select line is asserted and all other select lines have been de-asserted. Due to routing delays, some contention may still occur, but this circuit has reduced it significantly. Of course, the best solution may be to find better implementations. For example, designers can use

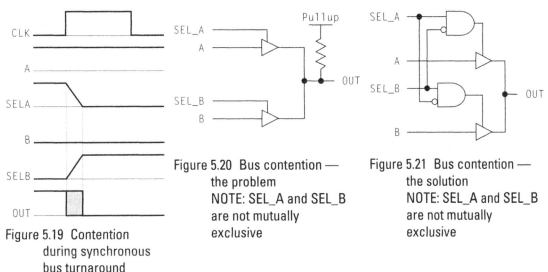

Figure 5.19 Contention during synchronous bus turnaround

Figure 5.20 Bus contention — the problem
NOTE: SEL_A and SEL_B are not mutually exclusive

Figure 5.21 Bus contention — the solution
NOTE: SEL_A and SEL_B are not mutually exclusive

muxes instead of tri-state drivers, though muxes are often difficult to implement in FPGAs. Other solutions involve designing the system so that there is always a clock cycle where nothing is driving the bus. Of course, during those cycles, you want to be certain that the bus does not float by pulling it up.

5.6 One-Hot State Encoding

For a typical "large-grained" FPGA architecture, the normal method of designing state machines is not optimal. This is because the normal approach to FSMs tends to couple a few flip-flops that encode state to a large network of combinatorial logic that decodes the state. In an FPGA, though, large combinatorial networks must be built by aggregating several CLBs. Each single CLB may contain small lookup tables that can easily implement any eight or nine input

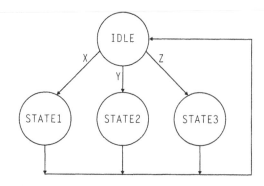

Figure 5.22 State diagram

combinatorial function. If you need a 10 input function, you need to spread the logic over two CLBs. Decoding the state representation used in classic FSM designs, can involve many CLBs. This means that routing becomes involved, significantly adding to the circuit delay, and slowing down the maximum clock speed for the design. An alternate design method, called one-hot state encoding, is better suited to FPGAs because it reduces the the number of inputs to the combinatorial network, thus reducing routing overhead and allowing better timing and thus faster clocks.

Figure 5.22 shows a small but typical state diagram for some simple state machine. Using the classic design methodology the four states would be represented as two state bits.

Figure 5.23 shows a typical design for this state machine, where the $(S1, S0)$ states are defined as follows: IDLE (00), STATE1 (01), STATE2 (10), and STATE3 (11). Notice that although the number of flip-flops are minimized, the combinatorial logic is fairly large. As the number of states grows, the number of inputs needed for the combinatorial logic grows because the state representation mustbe decoded to determine the current state.

The better method of designing state machines for FPGAs is known as one-hot encoding, shown in Figure 5.24. Using this method, each state is represented by a single state bit, thus a single flip-flop, rather than encoded from several state bits. This greatly reduces the combinatorial logic, because designers need to check only one bit to determine the current state. Many synthesis tools now recognize the need for one-hot encoding for FPGAs, and can re-encode your state bits to produce

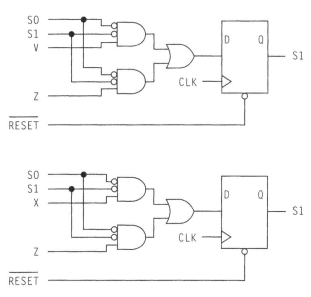

Figure 5.23 State machine: Usual method

optimal encoding for the particular CPLD or FPGA that you are using.

Note that each state bit flip-flop needs to be reset when initialized, except for the IDLE state flip-flop, which needs to be set so that the state machine begins in the IDLE state.

5.7 Design For Test (DFT)

The "Design for test" philosophy stresses that testability should be a core design goal. Designed-in test logic plays two roles. The first role is to help debug a chip that has design flaws. These flaws are problems where the chip may perform the function for which it is designed, but that design will not operate properly in your system. The second role of test logic is to catch physical problems. Physical problems usually show up in production, but sometimes marginal problems appear only after the chip has been in the field for some time. Sometimes the same test logic can fill for both roles. Sometimes, the two roles require different kinds of test structures.

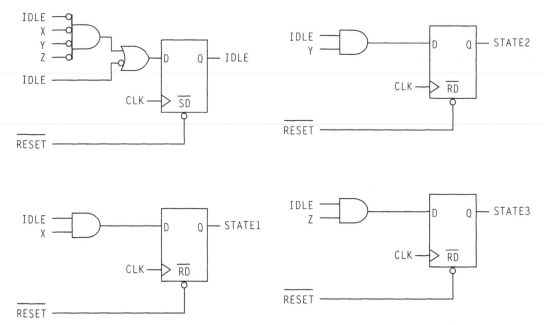

Figure 5.24 State machine: One-hot encoding

Both roles are particularly important for ASIC design because of the black box nature of ASICs, where internal nodes are simply not accessible when a problem occurs. These techniques are also applicable to CPLDs and FPGAs, many of which already have built-in test features. One difference between ASIC and FPGA/CPLD design is that for an ASIC design, you are expected to provide test structures and test vectors to use during production, to find any physical defects. With an FPGA, you can safely assume that the vendor has performed the appropriate production tests. However, some physical defects may show up only after prolonged use, so you may still want to design in test logic that allows you to check for physical defects while your chip is working in a system in the field. For each of the following tests, I note whether test is applicable to physical defects, functional problems, or both, and whether you can use the test for the debug process, in the field, or both.

- *Test circuitry should not make up more than 10 percent of the logic of the entire FPGA.*
- *You should not spend more than 10 percent of your time designing and simulating your test logic.*

Figure 5.25 The 10/10 rule of testing

5.7.1   The 10/10 Rule of Testing

While test logic is intended to increase the testability and reliability of your FPGA, if the test logic becomes too large, it can actually decrease reliability. This is because the test logic can itself have problems that cause the FPGA to malfunction. A rule of thumb that I call the 10/10 rule is described in Figure 5.25.

The following sections describe DFT techniques that allow for better testing of a chip. While not all of these techniques need to be included in every design, those techniques that are needed should be included *during the design process* rather than afterwards. Otherwise, circuits can be designed that are later found to be difficult, if not impossible, to test.

5.8 Testing Redundant Logic

5.8.1   What Is Redundant Logic?

Tests for	physical defects
It is used	in the field

Redundant logic is used most often in systems that need to operate continuously without failure. Military systems and banking systems are two examples of systems that should not stop while in use. In these types of systems, logic will be duplicated. There will be a device following the redundant hardware that compares the outputs of the redundant hardware. Often, these systems will have three redundant blocks so that if one block fails, two blocks are still working, and the one bad block can be ignored. The comparison hardware is called "voting" logic because it compares signals from the three redundant blocks and decides that the majority of signals that agree have the correct value.

Most hardware is not designed to continue to operate with a physical failure, so redundant logic is not common. However, if you do use redundant logic in your design, you want to make sure that all of the redundant logic is working correctly. The idea is that redundant logic finds manufacturing faults that occur

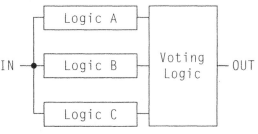

Figure 5.26 Redundant logic

after the chip is in the field. The next section discusses how to functionally test redundant logic.

Redundant Logic and the Battle Switch

Years ago, I worked for ROLM Corporation, the premiere Silicon Valley company of its day. ROLM was flying high, employing lots of people, and recording great revenue growth in the telecommunications industry. At the time, everyone wanted to work at ROLM. ROLM offered great salaries, stock option plans, and benefits. They epitomized the Silicon Valley workplace with large offices for engineers in spacious buildings on "campuses" that were nested among trees and artificial lakes. The cafeterias were subsidized by the company and served a great variety of foods in a quiet, elegant atmosphere. Most notably, the ROLM campus included a full health club with basketball courts, racquetball courts, weight room, swimming pool, Jacuzzi, and offered aerobics classes every day.

ROLM really defined the Silicon Valley company. It's sad that it grew too fast and didn't have the money to support the growth. It ended up being bought by IBM, split up, sold off in pieces, and eventually absorbed into several other companies. ROLM is a distant memory and most Silicon Valley engineers haven't even heard of it.

The reason I mention ROLM is that I worked in the Mil-Spec Computer Division, which manufactured computers for the military. We had to design fault tolerance and redundancy into the computers. On the side of our computers was a switch labeled the "battle switch," which no one really talked about. One day I asked a project leader about the function of this switch. He explained it this way. Throwing that switch turned off all error checking and fault tolerance. I asked him why. He replied that in a war, particularly a nuclear war, it's better to have a faulty computer fire off as many missiles as possible, even if some hit friendly targets, as long as one of them reaches the enemy. Pretty scary thought. I guess that's why no one discussed it, and I didn't either after that.

5.8.2   How to Test Redundant Logic

Tests for	functional problems
It is used	during debugging

Testing redundant logic is a separate issue. Figure 5.27 shows a circuit that has redundant logic. However, because the circuit is not testable, the effect is not as useful as it should be. If a design flaw exists, or a physical defect occurs before the chip is shipped, the redundant logic will hide the problem. If a defect occurs in the field, the chip will simply produce incorrect results — the incorrect redundant logic will not prevent failure. Thus, if it is to contribute meaningfully to reliability, redundant logic must properly tested before it is shipped.

The circuit in Figure 5.27 shows how modify Figure 5.26 for testing. The extra test lines allow you to disable some of the redundant logic and test each

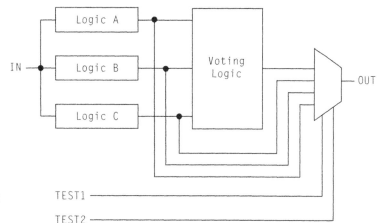

Figure 5.27 Testing redundant
logic

piece independently during debug of the design. This allows you to be sure that each piece of redundant logic is working correctly and identically with its redundant counterparts.

5.9 Initializing State Machines

Tests for	functional problems
It is used	during debugging

It is important that all state machines, and in fact all registers in your design, can be initialized. This ensures that if a problem arises, testers can put the chip into a known state from which to begin debugging.

Also, for simulation purposes, simulation software needs clocked devices to start in a known state. I like to use the example of a divide-by-two counter — i.e., a flip-flop with its Qn output tied to its D input. The output of this flip-flop is a square wave that is half the frequency of the input clock signal. It may not matter in the design whether the flip-flop starts out high or low. In other words, the phase relationship between the input clock and the half-frequency output clock may not matter. But when you simulate the design, the output clock will start out undefined. On the next clock cycle, the output will change from undefined to the inverse of undefined, which is ... undefined. The output clock will remain undefined for the entire simulation.

5.10 Observable Nodes

Tests for	functional problems
It is used	during debugging

It is a good idea to make internal nodes in your chip design observable. In other words, testers should be able to determine the values of these nodes by using the I/O pins of the chip. Figure 5.28a shows an unobservable state machine. In Figure 5.28b, the state machine has

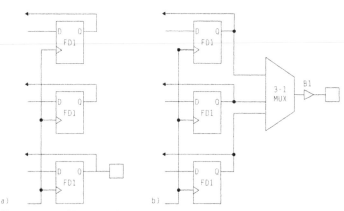

Figure 5.28 Observable nodes

been made observable by routing each state machine output through a mux to an external pin. Test signals can be used to select which output is being observed. If no pins are available, the state bits can be multiplexed onto an existing pin that, during testing, is used to observe the state machine. This configuration allows for much easier debugging of internal state machines. If your system includes a microprocessor, you can connect the microprocessor to the chip to allow it to read the internal nodes and assist with debugging.

5.11 Scan Techniques

Tests for	physical defects or functional problems
It is used	in the field or during debugging

Scan techniques sample the internal nodes of the chip serially so that they can be observed externally. Each flip-flop in the design gets replaced with a scan flip-flop, which is simply a flip-flop with a two-input mux in front of the data input as shown in Figure 5.29. The scan enable input (SE) is normally low, so that the normal data input gets clocked into the flip-flop. In scan mode, though, the scan enable input is high, causing the scan data (SD) to get clocked into the flip-flop.

The output of each flip-flop in the chip is then connected to the scan data input of another flip-flop, as shown in Figure 5.30. This creates a huge chain, called a scan chain. As discussed in detail in Chapter 7, Automatic Test Pattern Generation (ATPG) software packages take an HDL description and convert all flip-flops to scan flip-flops and insert the scan chain into your design.

There are two main scan techniques — *full scan* and *boundary scan*. Full scan involves creating scan chains from every flip-flop in the design. Boundary scan involves using only flip-flops that are connected to I/O pins in the scan chains.

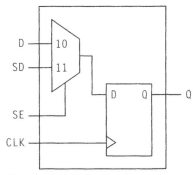

5.11.1 Full Scan

When performing full scan, the entire chip is put into scan mode, and the scan enable inputs to the scan flip-flops are asserted. Thus testers can examine the state of each flip-flop in the design. Also, testers can put the chip into a completely predictable state by scanning a certain pattern into it. This technique of scanning patterns into and out of the chip is used for finding physical defects in ASICs after production. In fact, it is the only practical way to catch defects in today's very large ASICs.

Figure 5.29 Scan flip-flop

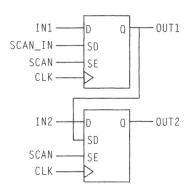

Figure 5.30 Scan Chain

Because FPGAs are not typically tested after production, except by the manufacturer, the use of scan is restricted to functional testing of FPGAs, if it is used at all. During debugging, if the chip malfunctions, it can be halted, put into scan mode, and the state of each flip-flop can be read via the scan. These bits can then be loaded into a simulation of the design to help figure out what went wrong. The simulation data can also be scanned back into the chip to put the chip into a known starting state. All of this allows the simulator and the physical chip to be used together to debug design problems — at least in theory.

The major problem with using this kind of technique for functional testing is that the scanning requires a lot of software development. Each flip-flop bit must be stored, and the software must know what to do with it. If the state is to be loaded into a simulator, there must be software to convert the state information to the simulator's format and back again. Also, if states are scanned into the chip, one must be careful not to scan in illegal states. For example, as bits are scanned into the chip, it is possible to turn on multiple drivers to a single net internally, which would normally not happen, but which would burn out the chip. Similarly, outputs must be disabled while the chip is being scanned because dangerous combinations of outputs may be asserted that can harm the attached system. There are other considerations, also, such as what to do with the clock and what to do with the rest of the system while the chip is being scanned. Avoiding these problems requires not only a certain level of sophistication in the software, may also require extra hardware. Only very large, expensive systems can justify the cost of full scan for most designs. Also, scan requires that the chip be halted, which may not be practical or even allowable in certain systems, such as communication systems or medical devices.

5.11.2 Boundary Scan

Boundary scan is somewhat easier to implement and does not add as much logic to the design. Boundary scan reads only nodes around the boundary of the chip, not internal nodes. Limiting the scan to boundary nodes avoids internal contention problems, but not contention problems with the rest of the system. Boundary scan is also useful for testing the rest of your system, because testers can toggle the chip outputs and observe the effect on the rest of the system. Boundary scan can be used to check for defective solder joints or other physical connections between the chip and the printed circuit board or between the chip and other chips in the system.

The Institute of Electrical and Electronic Engineers (IEEE) has created a standard for boundary scan called JTAG, or IEEE 1149.1. It covers pin definitions and signaling. Most CPLDs and FPGAs support this standard in their architecture, without the need for making any changes to your design.

5.12 Built-In Self-Test (BIST)

Tests for	functional problems
It is used	during debugging

Another method of testing a chip is to put all of the test circuitry on the chip in such a way that the chip tests itself. This is called built-in self-test, or BIST. In this approach, some circuitry inside the chip can be activated by asserting a special input or combination of inputs. This circuitry then runs a series of tests on the chip. If the result of the tests does not match the expected result, the chip signals that a problem exists. The details of what type of tests to run and how to signal a good or bad chip are dependent on several factors, including the type of circuit to be tested, the amount of area to be devoted to test logic, and the amount of time that can be spent on testing.

BIST can be used for production testing or in-field testing. Because CPLD and FPGA production testing is done by the manufacturer, its use for these devices is for in-field testing. BIST allows you to periodically test a device for physical defects while it is run-

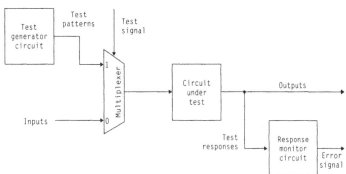

Figure 5.31 Built-in self-test

ning in the system, as long as there is an idle period where it is not in use. During those times, the chip can be commanded to run a test on itself. As mentioned in Chapter 4, commercial software is now available to add BIST circuitry to a design.

Figure 5.31 represents an entire chip, and shows, in general terms, how BIST is implemented. Your design is in the block labeled "circuit under test." Everything else is BIST logic. To put the chip into test mode, the external test signal is asserted. Then, all inputs to the circuit come from the test generator rather than the real chip inputs. The test generator circuit produces a series of test vectors that are applied to the circuit under test. The outputs of this circuit are then sent to a response monitor that compares the outputs to expected outputs. Any difference causes the error signal to be asserted.

One way to design the test generator is to store the simulation vectors in a memory and feed them out on each clock edge. The response monitor circuit would then also consist of a memory with all of the expected output vectors. The main problem, though, is that the memory to store the vectors would be too great, possibly even taking more silicon area than the original circuit. Another possibility would be to design logic to create the vectors and expected vectors, but that would require at least as much circuitry as the original chip design. The optimal solution is to use signature analysis, a form of BIST that is described in the next section.

5.13 **Signature Analysis**

Tests for	physical defects
It is used	in the field

A problem with the BIST technique, in general, is that the test generation and response monitoring circuitry can be extremely complex and take up a lot of silicon. Any test structure that is too large or complex ends up reducing the reliability of a design rather than increasing it, because now there is a significant chance that the test circuitry itself fails. Also, large test circuits increase the cost of a chip, another unwanted effect.

Signature analysis avoids these problems. BIST designs based on signature analysis use a test generation circuit that creates a pseudorandom sequence of test vectors. "Pseudorandom" means that the test vectors are distributed as though they were random, but they are actually predictable and repeatable. The response monitor takes the sequence of output vectors and compresses them into a single vector. This final compressed output vector is called the chip's signature. Although this type of testing is not exhaustive, if done right it can detect a very large number of failures. It is also possible that a nonworking chip will produce a correct signature, but if the number of bits in the signature is large, the probability of a bad device producing a good signature is very small.

Another significant advantage of signature analysis is that the pseudorandom number generation and the output vector compression can both be performed by a linear feedback shift register (LFSR), which is a very small device — simply a shift register and several XOR gates. Almost no silicon area is given up, and thus almost no additional cost is involved.

5.14 **Summary**

In this chapter, I have laid out specific design rules and guidelines that increase your chances of producing a working, reliable device — one that will work for different chip vendor processes and continue to work for the lifetime of your system. I have shown a number of examples of incorrect or inefficient designs, and the equivalent function designed correctly.

Specifically, after reading this chapter, you should be acquainted with these CPLD and FPGA design issues:

- Hardware description languages and different levels of design modeling.
- Top-down design, an approach to designing complex chips that allows you to better utilize or implement these important design capabilities:
  - Use of HDLs

- Written specifications
- Allocating resources
- Design partitioning
- Flexibility and optimization
- Reusability
- Floorplanning
- Verification

- The significance of architectural differences and how they affect design trade-offs.

- Synchronous design — A requirement for creating devices that will function reliably over their entire lifetimes.

- Floating nodes — A condition that must be avoided in order to avoid excess noise and power consumption.

- Bus contention — Another condition that must be avoided to increase the long-term reliability of your chip.

- One-hot state encoding — A method of designing state machines that takes advantage of the architecture of FPGAs.

- Testing redundant logic — Why it's important and the typical design structures for implementing such tests.

- Initializing state machines — Designing a chip so that all internal state machines are initialized.

- Observable nodes — Bringing internal nodes to external pins so that the internal states of the chip can be observed.

- Scan techniques — Connecting flip-flops inside the chip (either boundary nodes, or both boundary and internal nodes) into one or more chains so that you can easily get 100 percent fault coverage to guard against manufacturing problems.

- Built-in self-test (BIST) — A method of including circuitry inside a chip that lets it test itself for physical problems.

- Signature analysis — A method using linear feedback shift registers (LFSRs) to simplify BIST circuitry.

The Linear Feedback Shift Register

The LFSR is an extremely useful function that, I believe, would be used even more often if there were more good references showing how to design them. Most textbooks that cover LFSRs (and there aren't many), discuss the mathematical theory of primitive polynomials. Unfortunately, this view doesn't help an electrical engineer design one from flip-flops and logic. The two books that do have practical design information are *Designus Maximus Unleashed!* by Clive "Max" Maxfield and my book, *Verilog Designer's Library.* The first is a very fun, off-the-wall book with lots of design tips. The second offers a library of tested Verilog functions, including just about any LFSR you would want to design.

The LFSR uses a shift register and an exclusive OR gate to create a sequence of numbers that are pseudorandom. This means they look as though they were chosen at random. They're not truly random because the sequence is predictable, which is a good thing because for any kind of testing, we need to repeat an exact sequence of patterns.

The figure below shows a 3-bit LFSR. Notice that the inputs to the XOR must be from specific outputs of the shift register to create a sequence that covers all seven possibilities. These outputs are known as taps. If the taps are not in the right places, the sequence will repeat early and some patterns will never appear in the sequence. Also note that the value of zero is never in the sequence. Starting with a zero in the shift register will always produce a sequence of all zeroes. When the LFSR is initialized, the starting patterns must be some value other than zero. If you need to put a zero into the sequence, you can insert it with extra logic, but then the sequence is not truly random.

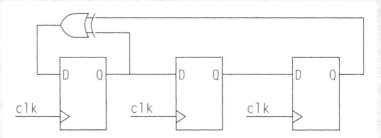

Figure 5.32 Linear feedback shift register

Using such an LFSR for the test generator and for the response monitor in a BIST circuit greatly simplifies the BIST circuit while still creating a chip signature that will flag most errors.

Exercises

1. The term HDL stands for
   (a) Hardware description language
   (b) High dollar lovin'
   (c) Hardware development language
   (d) High level design language

2. Match the model level on the left with the correct description on the right.

   (a) Algorithmic   A. Describes a design in terms of mathematical functionality.

   (b) Architectural   B. Describes a design in terms of basic logic, such as NANDs and NORs.

   (c) Register transfer level   C. Describes a design in terms of transistors and basic electronic components.

   (d) Gate level   D. Describes a design in terms of functional blocks.

   (e) Switch level   E. Describes a design in terms of Boolean logic and storage devices.

3. Which of the following HDL levels are considered behavioral levels?
   (a) Switch level
   (b) Algorithmic level
   (c) Gate level
   (d) Architectural level
   (e) Register transfer level

4. Which of the following HDL levels are considered structural levels?
   (a) Switch level
   (b) Algorithmic level
   (c) Gate level
   (d) Architectural level
   (e) Register transfer level

5. Select all of the statements that are true about top-down design.
   (a) Allows better allocation of resources
   (b) Allows each small function to be simulated independently
   (c) Speeds up simulations
   (d) Facilitates behavioral modeling of the device
   (e) Results in lower power consumption designs
   (f) Allows a design to be split efficiently among the various team members

6. Select the five rules of synchronous design.
   (a) Data signals must go only to combinatorial logic or data inputs of flip-flops.
   (b) All data is passed through combinatorial logic and flip-flops that are synchronized to a single clock.
   (c) Clocks cannot be gated — in other words, clocks must go directly to the clock inputs of the flip-flops without going through any combinatorial logic.
   (d) No combinatorial logic can have more than eight inputs.
   (e) Clock signals traces must be equal length to each flip-flop in the design.
   (f) No two logic gates can be connected together without a flip-flop between them.
   (g) All combinatorial logic must have a smaller delay than the worst-case setup time of the slowest flip-flop in the circuit.
   (h) No signal that is generated by combinatorial logic can be fed back to the same combinatorial logic without first going through a synchronizing flip-flop.
   (i) Delay is always controlled by flip-flops, not combinatorial logic.

7. Match each asynchronous circuit on the left with the equivalent synchronous circuit on the right.

(a)

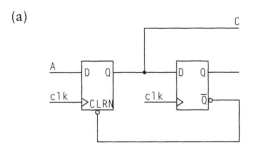

(A)

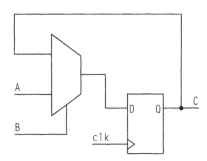

(b)

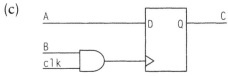

(B)

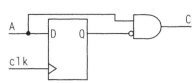

(c)

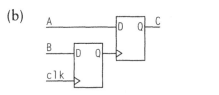

(C)

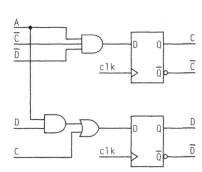

(d)

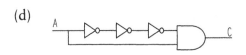

(D)

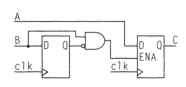

8. Select TRUE or FALSE for the following statements.
   (a) TRUE or FALSE: Synchronizing flip-flops are used to eliminate metastability.
   (b) TRUE or FALSE: In theory, a device can remain metastable forever.
   (c) TRUE or FALSE: The chances of a device going metastable increases with higher clock frequencies.
   (d) TRUE or FALSE: The chances of a device going metastable decreases with higher input voltage thresholds.
   (e) TRUE or FALSE: Schmidt trigger inputs with hysteresis can eliminate metastability.
   (f) TRUE or FALSE: Metastability is caused by faulty circuits.
   (g) TRUE or FALSE: Metastability is caused by asynchronous signals coming into synchronous circuits.

9. Check all allowable uses of asynchronous logic.
   (a) To latch inputs from and outputs to an asynchronous bus as long as the signals are synchronized for use inside the design.
   (b) For logic that must be extremely fast.
   (c) Asynchronous reset if it is done according to specific rules.
   (d) For designs that must save on power consumption.

10. Select TRUE or FALSE for the following statements:
    (a) TRUE or FALSE: Floating buses can create signal noise.
    (b) TRUE or FALSE: Floating buses can cause extra power consumption.
    (c) TRUE or FALSE: Floating buses should be avoided in your design.

11. Select all of the following circuits that avoid floating buses:

(a)

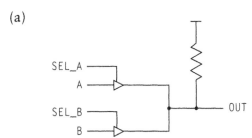

(b)

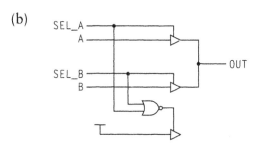

(c)

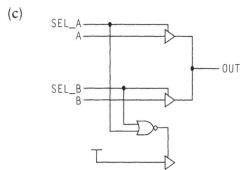

12. Select TRUE or FALSE for the following statements:
    (a) TRUE or FALSE: Bus contention can reduce the reliability of your design over its lifetime.
    (b) TRUE or FALSE: Bus contention should be minimized if it can't be eliminated entirely.

13. Select the circuit that has the greatest potential for bus contention.

(a)

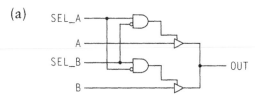

(b)

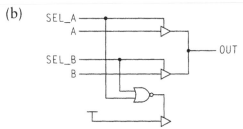

(c)

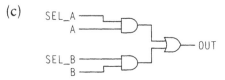

14. Testability should be considered (select one)
    (a) At the beginning of the design effort.
    (b) Around the middle of the design effort.
    (c) At the end of the design effort.

15. How many internal nodes in a design should be observable? (select one)
    (a) None
    (b) Half
    (c) All
    (d) As many as possible

16. Which one of these statements is true?
    (a) Scan chain insertion effectively turns an asynchronous design into a synchro-
         nous design for testing purposes.
    (b) Scan chain insertion effectively turns a complex design into a simple design for
         testing purposes.
    (c) Scan chain insertion effectively turns a sequential design into a combinatorial
         design for testing purposes.

17. Which of the following structures is not required for BIST?
    (a) Multiplexer
    (b) Response monitor
    (c) Linear feedback shift register (LFSR)
    (d) Test pattern generator

18. The 10/10 rule of testing is:
    (a) You should test 10 times every 10 days.
    (b) You should have 10 tests for every 10 percent of the design.
    (c) Testing circuitry should not up take more than 10 percent of the total circuitry and should not require more than 10 percent of the design and debug time.

In this chapter...

- *Defining verification*
- *Simulation*
- *Static timing analysis*
- *Assertion languages*
- *Formal verification*

Chapter 6

Verification

This chapter deals with verification, a group of methods and techniques used to detect design errors before a chip is created. This chapter describes the activities that are part of the verification process, including how to design testability into a chip and how to fully simulate a chip to ensure that it will function correctly in a completed system. The importance of and effort committed to verification is growing as CPLD and FPGA designs increase in size. In recent projects, I've found that more manpower is designated for verification than any other phase of the project. Also, all kinds of EDA tools are coming to the market to help with verification. Some of these tools are generic tools, and others are specifically for certain types of chips.

The EDA tools that enable many of the techniques in this chapter are described in detail in Chapter 7.

Objectives

- Understand the use of functional and multilevel simulation for catching design flaws
- Understand the need for regression testing to ensure that changes do not break the design.
- Learn how you can use static timing analysis to very quickly examine a design and determine the maximum frequency and flag all critical paths.

131

- Discover uses of assertion languages for simulation and formal verification.
- Learn where formal verification is appropriate and learn the difference between equivalency checking and functional verification.

6.1 What is Verification?

The term "verification" is a little nebulous. In the larger domain of IC design, "verification" generally refers to any technique that is used to verify that the chip will work correctly. These can include simulating the functionality of the chip, performing a timing analysis of the chip, running a formal verification of the design, emulating the chip, prototyping the chip, creating test vectors for automatic test equipment (ATE), writing software tests for in-system testing, and running long tests on the chip in the system. Not all of these techniques are applicable to programmable devices, though, and I cover only those that are applicable.

As chip sizes have grown large, in terms of gates and functionality, verification has become the part of the design process that usually requires the most time and manpower. Verification is an extremely important consideration in chip design because a chip cannot be blue-wired after production. For this reason, teams must perform simulation extensively before the chip is sent for fabrication. Verification has become an extremely important aspect of the design process that needs to be optimized.

6.2 Simulation

Perhaps the most important tool for chip verification is simulation. Simulation can save many frustrating hours debugging a chip in your system. Doing a good job at simulation uncovers errors before they are set in silicon, and can help determine that your chip will function correctly in your system.

Designers of programmable devices sometimes rush through or ignore the simulation phase of a design due to pressures to get a chip in a system. Sometimes the thinking is that the device will be placed in a board so that other members of the design team can debug the rest of the bug and so that software development can begin. Unfortunately, FPGAs in particular are very difficult to change once a pinout has been selected. FPGA software often has a difficult time placing logic within a chip and routing it when constraints exist. Pin placement is a definite constraint.

Also, skipping or postponing the simulation phase can result in a chip in your system that has significant problems. The engineers debugging the system or the software may end up fighting bugs in the chip that could have been discovered during simulation. My advice is to simulate a programmable chip as fully as possible before setting its pinout or committing it to a board.

Why Verify When I Can Reprogram?

One question that inevitably arises is "Why do I need to spend so much time simulating and verifying my design if I can simply reprogram the chip whenever I need to?" There are a lot of answers to this question. The first one is that verifying a chip extensively before putting it in a system is simply a smart thing to do. Problems with the chip can range from minor functional problems to major electrical problems that can potentially destroy the system in which it is used. A second answer is that a verification environment allows you to control every input to the device in very specific ways. This means that you can test functionality repeatedly until it is correct. You can create tests that exercise various functions of the chip in different situations. A real system rarely has this kind of controllability and repeatability. Finally, when a design is committed to a programmable device, and that device is soldered onto a circuit board, certain constraints are put on the design. Most notably, the pins of the device are then constrained to specific locations. The more constraints imposed on a specific design, especially I/O pin locations, the more difficult it is to make changes, even minor ones, to the placement and routing of the design. The placement and routing algorithms often have problems with small changes because the layout then becomes more difficult to optimize. Even when the placement and routing can be changed, the routing change is often accompanied by a significant change in the internal chip timing.

6.2.1 Functional Simulation

Functional simulation involves simulating the functionality of a device to determine that it is working the way the specification describes and that it will produce correct results within your system. This type of simulation is important initially in order to get as many bugs out of the device as possible and to determine that the chip will work correctly in your system.

When performing functional simulation, knowing how much simulation to perform and when to stop is sometimes difficult. It's not possible to simulate all possible combinations of inputs. One measure of simulation effectiveness, called code coverage, measures the percentage of the HDL statements that are exercised in all possible ways during simulation. As an example of "all possible ways," consider simulating an if-then statement. The simulation achieves full code coverage only if it simulates both conditions of the statement— one where the condition is true and the statement is executed, and one where the condition is false and the statement is not executed.

Some software tools calculate code coverage, and you should at least have 100 percent coverage before feeling good about the simulation. Even 100 percent coverage can still leave many potential faults uncovered, but it signifies that each state machine has been simulated and no part of the circuit has gone unexamined.

6.2.2 Multilevel Simulation

Because you have designed your chip using top-down methodology, you can take advantage of the multilevel simulation that can be achieved using HDLs. Your design will be created first using behavioral models that confirm the general algorithms and architecture of the chip. Then, behavioral functional blocks can be replaced with RTL descriptions. Finally, your design will be synthesized into a gate-level description.

The behavioral models will simulate very quickly (i.e., use up little computer processing time) because, by definition, behavioral models model only high level functions. Behavioral models shouldn't include clocks

> **Toggle Coverage**
>
> An older equivalence to code coverage, for schematic entry, was toggle coverage, which specified the percentage of nodes in the design that changed from a 1 to a 0 and from a 0 to a 1 at some time during the simulation. Toggle coverage is not used very much any more now that CPLDs and FPGAs are designed using HDLs rather than schematics.

and clock edges. As you refine different behavioral blocks into RTL descriptions, you can replace those behavioral blocks with their RTL equivalents and resimulate the design. This resimulation, with some behavioral blocks and some RTL blocks will take less computer resources and finish much faster than a full RTL simulation.

I strongly suggest that the person designing the behavioral block work independently from the person designing the same block in RTL. If the behavioral and RTL code are developed independently, when you substitute the RTL block for the behavioral block, you will not only test the functionality, you will test that the specification from which both blocks were designed is clear and precise. The designer of the behavioral block will make certain assumptions in the design. The RTL designer is unlikely to make those same assumptions unless they are supported by the specification. When the simulation is run on both cases, the results won't match, forcing you to examine those assumptions and decide which are correct.

The synthesis tools read the RTL as input and generate a gate level description as output. You can then simulate this gate level description and compare the results against the simulation of the RTL and behavioral level descriptions. This comparison serves two purposes. First, it tests that the synthesis program has performed correctly. Second, it ensures that you did not accidentally use a structure in your code that the synthesis software has misinterpreted.

Note that these simulations are typically self-checking. In other words, the simulation should check its own results for the correct output. Even so, you should hand check the first few tests to make sure that the checking code has been written correctly. Also, spot check simulations by hand from time to time to make sure that they are not passing off bad data as good.

Until basic flaws are eliminated and the basic functionality seems correct, the pieces of the design (especially of the RTL-level version) should be simulated as small independent blocks, each excercised separately from the entire design. This approach speeds up the debug process because each simulation will be concerned with only its small block of code and will not be affected by other blocks in the design – blocks that may or may not be working correctly. For these small scale simulations, it is reasonable to check for low-level functionality, for example, that specific events occur on specific clock edges. Once you have determined that the small block seems to be working, you can put it into the larger design and simulate the entire chip consisting of a combination of RTL and behavioral blocks.

The simulations of the entire chip should check for high-level functionality. For example, a simulation of an Ethernet switch might check that all incoming packets were retransmitted, though the simulation would probably not be concerned with the exact ordering or latency of the packets. Such a simulation would also not be checking for specific events on specific clock edges. As the design evolves, specific events may change, but the overall functionality should remain fairly constant.

6.2.3   Regression Testing

Regression testing involves repeatedly running a set of simulation tests on a design that has been modified, to ensure that the modifications have not introduced new bugs. Regression testing is often initiated after a designer has attempted to fix a bug or has added a new function to the design that may have inadvertently introduced errors. Regression tests are a quality control measure to ensure that the newly-modified code still complies with its specified requirements and that unmodified code has not been affected by the new code. With regard to the type of tests, regression tests typically represent the major functionality of the design and also several extreme situations known as "corner cases."

Corner cases are situations where extreme things are happening to the logic in the chip. Corner cases represent conditions most likely to make the chip fail. Examples of extreme cases include situations where an internal buffer gets filled and there is an attempt to write one more piece of data. Another example is an attempt to read an empty FIFO. Situations where several signals get asserted simultaneously could be a corner case. The designer is often a good person to determine some corner cases. On the other hand, outsiders (who bring fewer assumptions to the test process) can often come up with good tests for corner cases — tests that might not be obvious to the designer.

Regression tests, consisting of the main functional tests and corner case tests, are repeatedly run against the design to determine that it is working correctly. Whenever a new section of logic or other modification is completed the designers should run these tests again to determine that nothing broke. After synthesis, designers need to run the regression tests to determine that the synthesized design is functionally equivalent to the original design. Though formal verification programs, specifically for equivalence checking, are available that can logically compare two design descriptions for equivalence, designers typically use regression testing for anything other than minor changes to a design description. This is particularly true when a design has undergone major changes that make it similar but not identical to the previous design.

6.2.4 Timing Simulation

Timing simulations are simply functional simulations with timing information. The timing information allows the designer to confirm that signals change in the correct timing relationship with each other. There is no longer any reason to perform timing simulations on a fully synchronous design.

As chips become larger, this type of compute-intensive simulation takes longer and longer to run. Even so, these simulations cannot simulate every possible combination of inputs in every possible sequence; many transitions that result in problems will be missed. This means that certain long delay paths never get evaluated and a chip with timing problems can still pass timing simulation.

Instead, fully synchronous designs should be evaluated using a software tool called a static timing analyzer, which is described in the next section.

6.3 Static Timing Analysis

Static timing analysis is a process that examines a synchronous design and determines its highest operating frequency. Static timing analysis software considers the path from every flip-flop in the design to every other flip-flop to which it is connected through combinatorial logic. The tool calculates all best-case and worst-case delays through these paths. Any paths that violate the setup or hold timing requirements of a flip-flop, or that are longer than the clock period for a given clock frequency, are flagged. These paths can then be adjusted to meet the design requirements. Any asynchronous parts of the design (they should be few, if any) must be examined by hand.

6.4 Assertion Languages

Assertion languages are used to check properties of a design during simulation and during formal verification. Assertions allow designers to check that certain "invariant" properties or behaviors are consistently present. For example, a sequence of events that must always occur in a specific order could be checked with an assertion. These assertions may be legal or illegal conditions in the design. For example, a legal condition may be that all state machines are initialized when the reset signal is asserted. An illegal condition may be that two buffers are simultaneously driving a three-state bus.

For simulation, these tools allow you to check the inputs and outputs of a device, and often the internal states of the device. During simulation, these assertions confirm that events are occurring when they should, or they notify the user when illegal events occur or illegal states are entered by the design.

For formal verification, which I discuss in the next section, assertions are used for verifying that two design descriptions are equivalent by comparing the sequence of events and the internal states for both devices during simulation.

6.5 Formal Verification

Formal verification is the process of mathematically checking that a design is behaving correctly. There are two types of formal verification: equivalency checking and functional verification.

6.5.1   Equivalency Checking

Equivalency checking is the process of comparing two different design descriptions to determine whether they are equivalent. Design descriptions go through many different transformations. These include manual tweaking of a design by the design engineers, and also include the normal transformations required by the design process. Of these normal transformations, synthesis is the one that all designs must go through. Equivalency checking software can determine whether the RTL description that was input to the synthesis software is functionally equivalent to the gate level description that is output. Other types of transformations to the design occur when designers add BIST logic or scan logic, for example, or when designers perform any kind of automatic optimization. Equivalency checking is useful to make sure that functionality is not accidentally changed in any of these situations and, if an unintentional change occurs, the software can point the engineer to the malfunctioning part of the design.

6.5.2 Functional Verification

Functional verification is the process of proving whether specific conditions, called properties or assertions, occur in a design. These assertions may be legal or illegal conditions in the design. For example, a legal condition may be that a FIFO must assert the full signal when all locations in the FIFO have valid data. An illegal condition may be an assertion that the FIFO within a design can overflow. These assertions are written by an engineer, using an assertion language, as described in Section 6.4. A functional verification tool then determines, mathematically and rigorously, whether these condition could possibly occur under any legal situations. Functional verification tools must check that all legal assertions do occur and that all illegal assertions cannot occur.

6.6 Summary

This chapter defines one of the most significant, and resource consuming, steps in the design process — verification. Though simulation is central to most verification methods, the goal of this simulation is to test the functionality of the design, sometimes against the design specs, and sometimes against another version of the design. The major tools and strategies used in verification are:

- Functional simulation — Needed for verifying the correct functionality of your chip.

- Multilevel simulation — Simulation performed at different levels of abstraction — behavioral level, RTL, and gate level — in order to speed up the simulation effort, verify that your chip meets its specifications, and confirm that synthesis tools did not alter your design.

- Regression testing — Needed to confirm that all necessary functionality has been simulated and that any changes to your design have not affected previously simulated functionality.

- Timing simulation — Time consuming, inaccurate, and has been rendered obsolete by static timing analysis programs.

- Static timing analysis — Used to check the timing numbers for your design and verify that it will operate at the specified clock frequency or flag any paths that do not meet your timing requirements.

- Assertion languages — Enables you to set conditions and properties of your design in the HDL code so that software can determine whether these conditions can possibly be met and whether the properties are true.

- Formal verification — Allows you to mathematically verify the functionality of a design and verify that two design descriptions are functionally equivalent.

Exercises

1. What is meant by the term "functional simulation?"
   (a) Simulating how a design functions, without regard to timing
   (b) Simulating the functional equivalence of a design
   (c) Simulating the mathematical function that is represented by the design

2. What is meant by the term "toggle coverage?"
   (a) The number of nodes in a design that change state during simulation as a percentage of the total number of nodes
   (b) The number of nodes in a design that change state from 0 to 1 and from 1 to 0 during simulation as a percentage of the total number of possible state transitions
   (c) The number of nodes in a design that change state from 0 to 1 and from 1 to 0 during simulation as a percentage of the total number of nodes

3. What is meant by the term "code coverage?"
   (a) The percentage of code statements in a design that change state from 0 to 1 and from 1 to 0 during simulation as a percentage of the total number of code statements
   (b) The percentage of code statements in a design that have been executed during simulation
   (c) The percentage of code statements in a design that have been executed during simulation in every possible manner

4. What is meant by the term "timing simulation?"
   (a) A process that looks at a synchronous design and determines the highest operating frequency that does not violate any setup and hold times
   (b) A simulation that includes timing delays
   (c) A process that looks at an asynchronous design and fixes all critical paths to be within a certain time constraint

5. Why is timing simulation typically no longer done for a design?
   (a) Timing simulation does not produce accurate timing results.
   (b) Timing simulation software is not reliable.
   (c) Static timing analysis is a faster, more exhaustive analysis of whether a design meets its timing requirements.

6. What is meant by the term "static timing analysis?"

    (a) A process that looks at a synchronous design and determines the highest operating frequency that does not violate any setup and hold-times

    (b) A simulation that includes timing delays

    (c) A process that looks at an asynchronous design and fixes all critical paths to be within a certain time constraint

7. What are the two types of formal verification?

    (a) Functional verification and equivalency checking

    (b) Functional checking and equivalency timing

    (c) Static verification and dynamic verification

    (d) Functional checking and equivalency verification

In this chapter...

- *Software tools for simulation*
- *Tools for synthesis, formal verification, place and route, and floorplanning*
- *Testbench, scan insertion, and built-in self-test (BIST) generators*
- *In situ and programming tools*
- *Static timing analysis*

Chapter 7

Electronic Design Automation Tools

Electronic design automation (EDA) tools are an extremely important factor in the design of CPLDs and FPGAs. Initially, PAL vendors and manufacturers of desktop devices for programming PALs provided some very simple HDLs for creating simple designs. Special simulation tools were created to simulate these simple programmable devices. EDA tool vendors added simple features that allowed engineers to use the tools to develop these simple devices.

When more complex devices, CPLDs and FPGAs, arrived on the scene, schematic capture tools were adapted to create designs for these devices. When the tools did not provide the design engineer with enough features to take advantage of device architectures that were growing in complexity, CPLD and FPGA vendors created their own tools.

Eventually, two realizations among programmable device vendors and EDA software tool vendors changed the landscape for these software tools. First, device vendors realized that better, cheaper tools sold their products. When an engineer was deciding on a device to use in his design, the software tools for enabling that design were often just as important as the architecture, size, and technology of the device itself. The device vendors that discovered this fact too late were relegated to the role of niche players; many of them are now out of business or still trying to catch up to the big players.

141

The other realization, by the software tool vendors, was that these new devices needed their own set of tools in order to take full advantage of their technologies and architectures. It wasn't good enough to simply add switches and parameters to existing tools. This realization came late to some of the big EDA companies, allowing smaller startups to establish themselves in this new, growing market.

Objectives

- Learn how to evaluate and choose appropriate software tools to simplify and expedite the design process.
- Understand and utilize testbench and built-in self-test (BIST) generators to test your chip during the design process.
- Learn about other tools and techniques to aid in your chip design.

7.1 Simulation Software

Simulation software allows you to exercise the functionality of a design in order to test whether it will work correctly in the intended system. Many vendors provide simulation software. Because CPLD and FPGA designs are now commonly created using an HDL, as are ASICs, you can use the same simulation tools for any of these devices.

Ironically simulators use four signal values to simulate binary logic. First are the two binary states of 1 and 0. However, because the goal is to simulate real hardware, not ideal logic circuits, the simulator tracks non-ideal states as well. The two additional states typically are represented by the symbols Z and X. A Z or "floating" signal represents a high impedance value. When no device is driving a a signal line, the line will be assigned the value Z. An X represents an undefined state. When the simulator cannot determine which of the other three states to assign to the signal, it will mark it X. This usually means that there is a problem with the design. An X state could mean that two devices are simultaneously driving a signal and that one device is attempting to drive it to a 1 value while the other device is attempting to drive it to a 0 value.

Some simulators also have additional states that can be assigned to signals to distinguish specific undefined states or to give the user more information about the hardware that is driving a signal. The high output of a buffer may be given a value that represents a "strong" 1, whereas a pull-up resistor on a signal may be assigned a value that represents a "weak" 1. However, with a digital circuit, especially in an FPGA where the user has little control over the specific hardware used to implement a logic function, these intermediate values give only marginal extra information and are rarely used.

Simulators also have the capability to aggregate signals into buses and represent them as numbers. For example, simulators can aggregate eight signals into a single 8-bit number and represent it in hex or decimal. This capability makes it easier to view buses as bytes or addresses, but has no effect on the actual operation of the circuit.

Altera Catches Up To Xilinx

Xilinx was the inventor of the FPGA, and for years was the only company offering these devices in any significant numbers. Xilinx had easily captured the small but growing FPGA market. As the market grew, CPLD vendors began to offer their own FPGAs, but Xilinx was able to maintain about a 70 percent market share for a number of years.

Then along came Altera. Altera had been successfully selling CPLDs for years when it entered the FPGA market with its own device. As you will see in Section 7.10, place and route software is typically supplied by the FPGA vendor. Xilinx had been providing a place and route tool and charging a pretty high price for it. Their philosophy was that Xilinx was the market leader, and thus the majority of engineers needed their version of the tool and should pay for it. Altera realized that it could use the software tools to sell the hardware. After all, they were a hardware company — not a software company. So Altera created a nice integrated package of EDA tools and offered it at a very low price. Engineers loved it, and for the first time in years, a company was able to take market share away from Xilinx.

A personal example of how well this strategy worked was that when Altera started offering their tools, I got a phone call from a local representative. She told me that consultants were being given the entire software package for free and they just needed my shipping address. They realized that I would gain expertise in their tools, recommend their parts in designs, and they would sell more chips.

I called up Xilinx and told them about this deal. I explained that when a client called me up to do a design I could tell them that I could start on an Altera design today, or the client could purchase the Xilinx tools and I could learn them and start the design in a couple of weeks. Which vendor do you think the client would chose? The Xilinx sales rep said they would choose the market leader and offered me a 50 percent discount on the tools, which I turned down.

Several years later, when Altera had actually surpassed Xilinx in market share, Xilinx woke up and began producing much better software at competitive prices. In fact, I later talked to an application engineer at Xilinx and once again mentioned that Altera had given me their tools for free. The next day I found a package at my doorstep containing a full suite of Xilinx software.

Listing 7.1 shows Verilog code for verifying a circuit that performs a cyclic redundancy check (CRC). Note that the code in the figure does not perform the CRC itself. The code in the figure consists of a module called crc_sim() that tests that some other module, called crc(), performs a CRC correctly. This crc_sim() module is called a testbench because it applies stimuli to a hardware design to test whether the hardware design works correctly. The crc_sim() testbench module and the crc() hardware module are compiled together and then simulated together. I do not expect you to understand the details of the Verilog code — that is beyond the scope of this book — but notice the $display statements in the code. These statements allow text to be output to the screen during simulation in order to debug the design.

Listing 7.1   CRC generator testbench

```
/************************************************************/
// MODULE:        CRC simulation
//
// FILE NAME:     crc_sim.v
// VERSION:       1.0
// DATE:          January 1, 1999
// AUTHOR:        Bob Zeidman, Zeidman Consulting
//
// CODE TYPE:     Simulation
//
// DESCRIPTION:   This module provides stimuli for simulating
// a CRC generator/verifier. It creates a large, random,
// frame of data which is shifted through an LFSR to produce
// an FCS which is appended to the frame. In every even
// frame, a single bit is corrupted. Each frame, with the
// appended FCS, is then shifted through the LFSR again. For
// uncorrupted frames, the LFSR is expected to contain zero
// at the end. For corrupted frames, the LFSR is expected to
// have a non-zero value.
//
/************************************************************/


// DEFINES
`define FCS 8                          // Number of bits in the fcs
`define FRAME 128                      // Number of bytes in the frame
```

Listing 7.1   CRC generator testbench (Continued)

```verilog
`define BFRAME (`FRAME*8)            // Number of bits in the frame
`define TOT_BITS (`BFRAME+`FCS)      // Total number of bits
                                     // including frame and FCS
`define FRAME_CNT 16                 // Number of frames to test


// TOP MODULE
module crc_sim();


// INPUTS


// OUTPUTS


// INOUTS


// SIGNAL DECLARATIONS
reg                 clk;
reg                 reset;
wire                bit_in;
wire [`FCS-1:0]     fcs;

integer             cycle_count;     // Counts clock cycles
integer             frame_count;     // Counts frames
reg  [`TOT_BITS-1:0] frame_data;     // Frame data bits
reg                 gen_check;       // Generate/check CRC
                                     // = 1 to generate CRC
                                     // = 0 to check CRC
integer                              // Temporary variable


// PARAMETERS


// ASSIGN STATEMENTS
assign bit_in = frame_data[cycle_count];


// MAIN CODE
```

Listing 7.1   CRC generator testbench (Continued)

```verilog
// Instantiate the CRC logic
CRC crc(      .clk(clk),
      .reset(reset),
      .bit_in(bit_in),
      .fcs(fcs));

// Initialize inputs
initial begin
   clk = 0;
   reset = 1;                    // Reset the FCS
   gen_check = 1;                // Generate FCS
   cycle_count = `TOT_BITS - 1;
   frame_count = `FRAME_CNT;

   // Initialize random number generator
   frame_data = $random(0);

   // Create random frame data of `FRAME bytes
   for (i = 0; i < `FRAME; i = i + 1) begin
      frame_data = (frame_data << 8) | (($random) % 256);
   end
   // Then shift it left `FCS places
   frame_data = frame_data << `FCS;
end

// Generate the clock
always #100 clk = ~clk;

// Simulate
always @(negedge clk) begin
   // If reset is on, turn it off
   if (reset)
      reset = 0;
   else begin
      if (cycle_count == 0) begin
```

Listing 7.1   CRC generator testbench (Continued)

```
if (gen_check) begin
   // Begin the CRC check
   gen_check = 0;
   cycle_count = `TOT_BITS - 1;

   // Put the FCS at the end of the data stream
   frame_data[`FCS-1:0] = fcs;

   // Corrupt one bit one every other test
   if ((frame_count & 1) == 0) begin
      $display("Corrupting frame");

      // Choose a random bit to corrupt
      i = {$random} % (`TOT_BITS);
      frame_data = frame_data ^ (`TOT_BITS'h1 << i);
   end

   // Reset the FCS
   reset = 1;
end
else begin
   if (((frame_count & 1) !== 0) &&
      (fcs !== `FCS'h0)) begin
      $display("\nERROR at time %0t:", $time);
      $display("CRC produced %h instead of 0\n", fcs);

      // Use $stop for debugging
      $stop;
   end
   else if (((frame_count & 1) == 0) &&
      (fcs == `FCS'h0)) begin
      $display("\nERROR at time %0t:", $time);
      $display("CRC passed a bad frame\n", fcs);

      // Use $stop for debugging
      $stop;
```

Listing 7.1   CRC generator testbench (Continued)

```
                end
            else begin
                $display("CRC #%d passed",
                    `FRAME_CNT-frame_count);

                // Reset the FCS
                reset = 1;
            end

            if (frame_count == 0) begin
                $display("\nSimulation complete - no errors\n");
                $finish;
            end
            else begin
                // Start the next frame
                frame_count = frame_count - 1;
                cycle_count = `TOT_BITS - 1;
                gen_check = 1;

                // Create random frame data of `FRAME bytes
                for (i = 0; i < `FRAME; i = i + 1) begin
                    frame_data = (frame_data << 8) |
                        (($random) % 256);
                end
                // Then shift it left `FCS places
                frame_data = frame_data << `FCS;
            end
        end
    end
    // Decrement the cycle count
    cycle_count = cycle_count - 1;
  end
end
endmodule           // crc_sim
```

Figure 7.1 shows the output from the simulation of the CRC generator. Note that the HDL syntax includes statements that output information to the screen. What you see displayed, whether it consists of text comments or signal and bus values, is controlled by the HDL code. The text that is displayed can be very useful for debugging purposes, but has no effect on the actual design of the chip.

The simulation tools typically have graphic interfaces that allow you to view inputs, outputs, and internal signals, buses, and states as waveforms. These waveforms are very useful for quickly visualizing and understanding the relationship between different signals being simulated. A sample simulation waveform from the simulation of the CRC generator is shown in Figure 7.2.

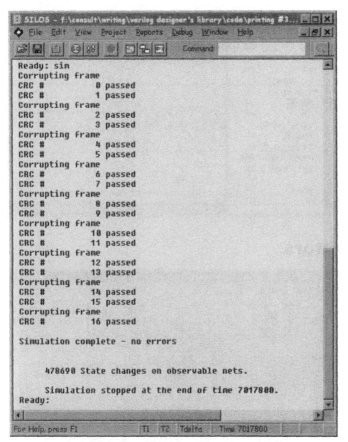

Figure 7.1   Sample text output from SILOS® simulation software (copyright 2002, by Simucad Inc.)

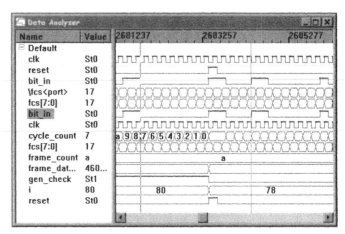

Figure 7.2   Sample simulation waveform output from SILOS® simulation software (copyright 2002, by Simucad Inc.)

7.2 Testbench Generators

When simulating a chip design, you need to apply signals to the design in order to examine how the chip responds. To evaluate the result, you need to compare the output of the simulation to the output you expect from a correct design. The code that generates the stimulus to the design and examines the outputs of the design is called a testbench. As designs get larger and more complex, testbenches become more difficult to design. For

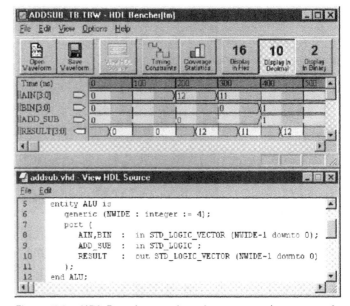

Figure 7.3   HDL Bencher testbench generator (courtesy of Xilinx Inc.)

example, a chip that implements a 24-port gigabit Ethernet switch might require a testbench that generates random sized packets containing random data and transmits them into each of the 24 ports at random intervals. The testbench would also need to examine those packets as they leave the switch to ensure that all packets were transmitted without error or with an acceptable error rate.

Testbench generators are software tools that help you write these testbenches quickly and efficiently. These generators vary according to the application. One testbench generator may be a scripting language that creates HDL code to generate test vectors and examine outputs. Another test generator may generate a file of random inputs to the design, allowing you to capture the outputs for manual examination. Some testbench generators may capture input data from a real system so that you can play it back and apply it to a simulated design.

Figure 7.3 presents a screen shot of one testbench generator, the HDL Bencher program from Xilinx.

7.3 In Situ Tools

A relatively new type of tool, which I call an "in situ" tool, allows a simulation, emulation, or prototype of a device to exchange data with real hardware, or a real system, as if the simulated, emulated, or prototyped device were a real physical device. For example, the simulated switch described in the preceding section could be connected to a real network and actually direct traffic on that network. Of course, the simulated device would run many times slower than the real device, slowing down

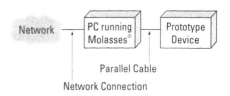

Figure 7.4   Diagram of in situ tool Molasses connecting a prototype to a live network. (courtesy of Zeidman Consulting)

the network considerably. If design teams use this technique correctly, though, they can discover many corner cases and real performance bottlenecks that they wouldn't otherwise find until after they had programmed the device, soldered it into a circuit board, and used it in a real system under real conditions. An example of the use of one such in situ tool is shown in Figure 7.4. In this figure, Molasses® is software running on a PC that allows an FPGA-based design to connect to a network at full speed, even though the FPGA-based design may only run at a fraction of the speed required by the network.

7.4 Synthesis Software

Synthesis software is used to translate an RTL design into a gate level design that can be mapped to logic blocks in the programmable device. Synthesis software allows you to write code at a much higher level than would otherwise be possible. Rather than designing a device in terms of NAND and NOR gates, you can design it using Boolean equations and high level devices such as counters, ALUs, decoders, and microprocessors. Also, the synthesis software optimizes the design for the particular device from the particular vendor that you specify. Synthesis software frees the designer from the need to understand details about the chip architecture. Synthesis software is what makes RTL-coded designs portable across device to device and vendor to vendor.

As shown in Figure 7.5, RTL code is input to the synthesis software, which creates an equivalent gate level description that is then input to the place and route software. The place and route software, described in Section 7.10, then creates a physical layout. In the case of

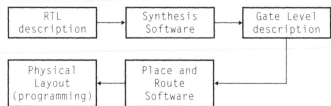

Figure 7.5   Diagram showing synthesis and place and route

CPLDs and FPGAs, the physical layout is represented by the bits that are used to program the device.

Often the synthesis software is a push-button operation, as Figure 7.6 shows. You specify the design input files, push the run button, and a gate level description is created. For some designs that push the limits of gate count or timing, you will need to set parameters for the program. These parameters are available as check boxes and menu selections on different screens of the synthesis software. These parameters may tell the program to optimize for density or speed, for example. You may be able to set switches that determine which types of optimization algorithms to use so that you can test different ones on your design.

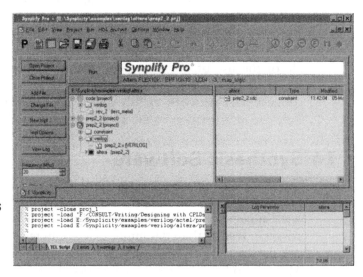

Figure 7.6   Symplify™ synthesis software (courtesy of Synplicity, Inc., use with permission)

You will often need to write your HDL code in very specific ways so that the synthesis software can understand it. Like with any coding language, there are many different ways to describe the same function or hardware structure. The synthesis tools often require the designer to limit the code descriptions to a well-defined coding style so that the synthesis tool does not need to search as many possibilities to figure out what you intended. The Verilog and VHDL standards specify subsets of each language that are supported by synthesis programs.

Within this synthesis-friendly subset of the HDL, there are still many different ways to describe a function or hardware structure. Some synthesis tools produce good results regardless of the language constructs that you use. Some synthesis tools are timing constraint driven and automatically decide which parts of your design should be optimized to save gates and which parts must be sped up to meet your timing requirements.

Other tools perform less optimization, requiring even more information from the designer. In this case, you may be required to try out different synthesis algorithms on different pieces of hardware. Or you may need to specify which critical paths need to be optimized to get the best timing, and which pieces of logic need to be optimized to minimize the number of gates. In these cases, you will need to add comments with a very specific format that informs the synthesis software how to do its job. These comments that are used by the synthesis program are called "pragma."

Some synthesis tools allow you to use a scripting language in order to optimize your design. The advantage of a scripting language is that it does not require you to make changes to your HDL code and it allows you to repeat the optimizations after you make design changes.

7.5 Automatic Test Pattern Generation (ATPG)

Automatic test pattern generation (ATPG) is a software tool for automatically generating simulation test vectors based on the design description. The vectors generated by ATPG are usually chosen for their contribution to fault coverage, a means for finding manufacturing defects in a device. Because the CPLD or FPGA vendors test their chips after production and before shipping them, ATPG is not typically used for designing programmable devices.

7.6 Scan Insertion Software

As I discussed in Section 5.11, you can link flip-flops into scan chains for testability reasons. Full scan is not commonly used in programmable devices and boundary scan is usually built into the part using a standard JTAG interface. However, some EDA vendors offer scan insertion software that will take the flip-flops in your HDL code and insert the appropriate logic to create scan chains and the control for the scan chains. This additional logic doesn't affect the function of your chip, although it will change the timing slightly. These tools are more commonly used for ASICs than CPLDs or FPGAs.

7.7 Built-In Self-Test (BIST) Generators

Another method of testing your chip is to put all of the test circuitry on the chip in such a way that the chip tests itself. This is called built-in self-test or BIST,

Synplicity vs. Synopsys

Synopsys was the inventor of synthesis software and was by far the powerhouse EDA company in this area for many years. Synopsys targeted its software at ASIC designs, initially a much bigger market than CPLDs and FPGAs. As CPLDs and FPGAs became more complex and required synthesis tools, Synopsys added switches to its software to allow it to optimize its results better for FPGAs. Two friends of mine, Ken McElvain and Alisa Yaffa, realized that this kluge method of synthesis could not produce optimal results for the unique architectures of CPLDs and FPGAs and formed their own company for targeting specific vendor chips. In other words, to synthesize a design for a specific chip from a specific vendor, the synthesis software needed to understand that specific architecture.

Synopsys initially scoffed at the idea. But not for long as Synplicity grabbed market share away from them in what was becoming a very important, and large, market. An example of how well the Synplicity concept worked comes from my personal experience. I was designing some bus controller CPLDs for an ATM router at Cisco Systems. I worked late into the evening attempting to get Synopsys Design Compiler software to synthesize my design into the CPLD I had chosen. I was changing parameters and switches in the software, and though I knew instinctively that the chip had more than enough resources, I couldn't get the Synopsys software to do it. At this time, Synplicity consisted of two employees – Ken and Alisa – in a very small office. At about ten o'clock in the evening I called up Ken, who was of course still working also, and explained my dilemma. He told me to e-mail him my HDL code along with the vendor and chip that I was targeting, and he'd see what his beta software could do. Twenty minutes later I received an e-mail back that included a fitted design with a clock speed that was faster than the Synopsys results. Knowing only the chip architecture, the Synplicity software was able to optimize and fit the design. Cisco management was impressed enough to invite them in for a demo and eventually became a major customer. After a while, Synopsys realized that it needed better tools for CPLDs and FPGAs if it was going to compete in this market.

described in Section 5.12. BIST software tools can automatically add the test generator circuit and response monitor circuit to your design (refer to Figure 5.31), along with the logic for switching between normal operation and test mode. The type of circuits that the software adds will depend on the function that your device performs. BIST circuitry for memory type devices usually generates specific patterns, such as walking ones or checkerboard tests. BIST circuitry for devices implementing control logic usually use linear feedback shift registers (LFSRs) for generating test inputs and for creating a response monitor circuit that produces a signature that is specific for the design.

7.8 Static Timing Analysis Software

Static timing analysis is a process that examines a synchronous design and determines its highest operating frequency, as described in Chapter 6. Currently available static timing analysis software can very quickly perform a static timing analysis on an entire chip design. Note that you must examine by hand any asynchronous parts of your design (they should be few, if any).

Figure 7.7 shows an example of the static timing analysis software supplied with the Quartus® II package from Altera Corporation. The user simply points to the design and specifies the particular device family, as shown. The timing

Figure 7.7 Quartus® II static timing analysis software (courtesy of Altera Corporation)

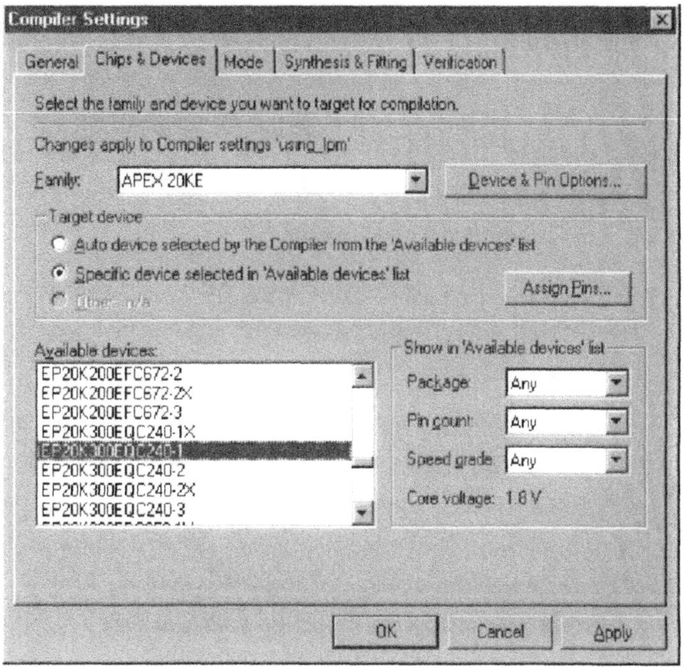

numbers depend on which device the design uses. The software loads the timing numbers for the device, which it gets from a vendor-supplied database. It then goes through you're the candidate (synchronous) design and examines each path between flip-flops to produce a very accurate timing analysis.

Before static timing analysis tools were available, engineers used timing simulation to verify the timing of designs. Timing simulation involves simulating the functionality of a design by using accurate timing values in the simulation. Delays from one signal to another could be viewed in a waveform. Timing problems became apparent when borderline timing caused flip-flop outputs to go

NeoCAD

To my knowledge, there has only been one attempt at producing generic place and route software for use on FPGAs from different vendors. Years ago, a few software engineers out of Xilinx formed a company called NeoCAD. These engineers had created the place and route software for Xilinx and decided that they would form a business based on a model like those of the simulation and synthesis software companies. In other words, they would produce generic place and route software that customers could fine tune for chips from different FPGA vendors. In this way, customers would not be obligated to use layout tools from the particular vendor. It would also make FPGA designs a little more portable from vendor to vendor.

They started, of course, with tools for Xilinx. These tools were very good — in fact, they usually outperformed the tools from Xilinx. They had a problem, though, with their business model. The place and route tools require an intimate knowledge of the vendor's architecture, and most vendors considered this proprietary information that they weren't interested in sharing. Some small FPGA companies were willing to give this information to NeoCAD in the hopes that NeoCAD would expand their customer base. The big players weren't willing to do this. Xilinx was particularly unhappy and made a point of withholding this information.

NeoCAD, with their intimate knowledge of Xilinx architecture, was able to continue to write place and route tools for Xilinx FPGAs that actually outperformed the Xilinx tools. For other vendors, they were not quite as successful.

One day I met a software engineer who had recently left Xilinx. He told me that the head of software there was pretty upset that NeoCAD, with their lack of detailed, up-to-date knowledge of the Xilinx architecture, could still create tools that outperformed Xilinx. He gave his team an ultimatum. Either the next toolset outperforms NeoCAD or they'd all be fired. Well, they worked hard and came out with a new place and route tool. Several months later, Xilinx purchased NeoCAD and had a new team of software engineers and a new place and route tool.

undefined. Signals that extended beyond one clock cycle into the next caused serious functionality problems. The drawbacks to timing simulation are three-fold: the timing simulations take a lot of computing power and thus a lot of time to complete; the results often require much direct examination of waveforms to find problems; and, marginal problems in a path where the simulation did not exercise all possible transitions, are very easy to miss. In the days when designs were less than 10,000 gates, timing simulation was a tedious process that often missed many marginal paths. With the sizes of modern designs, timing simulation simply doesn't work.

7.9 Formal Verification Software

Formal verification software mathematically checks that a design is behaving correctly. There are two types of formal verification: equivalency checking and functional verification. Equivalency checking software compares two different design descriptions to determine whether they are equivalent. Functional verification software proves whether specific conditions, called properties or assertions, occur in a design. Both types of formal verification are described in more detail in Section 6.5.

7.10 Place and Route Software

The vendor usually provides the place and route software tools. These tools take the gate level design created by the synthesis software and figure out which logic blocks in the chip should contain which logic and how they should be connected. This process is shown in the diagram in Figure 7.5. The place and route software next determines the bit sequence that will be loaded into the device in order to program each logic block and each routing connection to obtain the correct functionality. A screen shot of software from Actel Corporation, called Designer, is shown in Figure 7.8. The button labeled "Layout" initiates the place and route function; the button labeled "Fuse" creates the file containing the bit pattern for programming the device.

Different vendors use different algorithms for their place and route software in order to optimize the final design. Some vendors use a deterministic algorithm; others use a random seed algorithm. A deterministic algorithm uses a specific, unchanging method to determine optimal placement and routing. The advantage of a deterministic algorithm is that the results are identical each time it is used. The deterministic algorithm needs to be carefully designed and implemented in order to produce good results, especially for large, com-

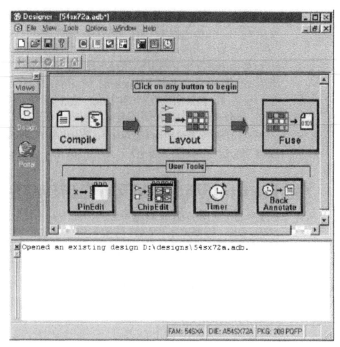

Figure 7.8   Designer place and route software (copyright 2002 by Actel Corporation)

plex designs. The random seed algorithm produces a random number that is used to select circuits for placement and routing. This type of algorithm produces a new layout each time it is run. Typically random seed tools can be run multiple times; each run will compare the new result against the previous one and keep the best result. Each new run can keep sections of the layout that have good timing and density and retry only the sections that did not produce good results. The advantage of a random seed algorithm is that it does not need to be a perfect algorithm to produce good results. The disadvantage is that it may run through a large number of iterations before it finds acceptable results.

7.10.1 Floorplanning Tools

Floorplanning is the process of placing large functional blocks in your design at specific places on the chip before any place and route occurs. The idea is that as chips become larger, design tools need help placing the various functions in the device. By floorplanning ahead of time, you are using your skills as the designer to help the place and route software. Essentially by tying certain blocks to certain locations on the chip die, you give the place and route software a much easier job. It now has to optimize the layout for several medium-sized blocks rather than one large block.

Floorplanning software is often part of the place and route software. It can also be a separate tool. Whether floorplanning will help you get a better layout in a shorter amount of time really depends on the function of your design, its size, its complexity, the regularity of the logic, how well you understand the design, and the effectiveness of the place and route software.

7.11 Programming Tools

Programming a device is a fairly simple procedure. Reprogrammable devices, such as SRAM-based FPGAs, are programmed in the system. The system must be designed in such a way that it knows how to program the device. In most cases, a small serial EEPROM memory is loaded with the appropriate bit pattern (the pattern generated by the place and route software). This serial EEPROM is connected to the FPGA, and when the system is powered on, circuitry within the FPGA automatically provides the appropriate handshaking to load the data from the serial PROM, programming itself. Once this operation is complete, the FPGA begins functioning as you designed it. A typical connection between the FPGA and a serial EEPROM is shown in Figure 7.9.

Figure 7.9   Serial EEPROM for programming FPGA (courtesy of Atmel Corporation)

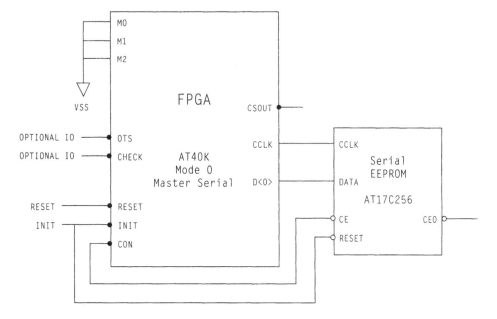

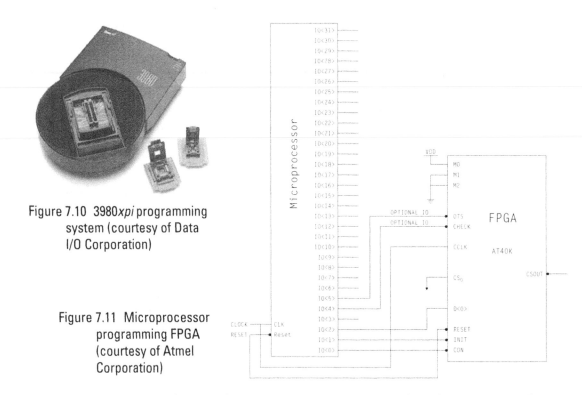

Figure 7.10 3980*xpi* programming system (courtesy of Data I/O Corporation)

Figure 7.11 Microprocessor programming FPGA (courtesy of Atmel Corporation)

Another technique for programming an SRAM-based FPGA is to have a microprocessor in the system write the programming data into the FPGA. In this way, designers can easily make modifications to the design by loading new programming files into the system and having the microprocessor load the new programming into the FPGA. A typical connection between the FPGA and a microprocessor is shown in Figure 7.11.

Blank one-time programmable devices, such as most CPLDs and antifuse FPGAs, are programmed using a device programmer that physically holds the chip, such as the one shown in Figure 7.10 from Data I/O Corporation. The operator points the programmer software to the program file produced by the place and route software and tells it to write the program. In a short time, the programmed device is ready.

7.12 Summary

This chapter discussed the currently available software tools that you may need to complete an CPLD or FPGA design. Here is a list of those tools and how they can help you during the design process:

- Simulation tools allow you to test the functionality of your design under normal conditions and under extreme conditions.
- Testbench generators automatically generate simulation testbenches from a simple test description.
- In situ tools enable you to connect your simulation, emulation, or prototype to a live system for testing.
- Synthesis tools enable you to design your chip at a very high level and then synthesize it into a low level design for place and route.
- Automatic test pattern generation (ATPG) tools automatically create test inputs to your chip for simulation or testing of the physical chip.

Floorplanning

Years ago, in the early days of ASICs, floorplanning was touted as a way to use human intelligence and experience to assist layout software for creating optimal layout. The concept of floorplanning is that a design engineer specifies where to place particular function blocks of a chip on the chip die. The software can then place the remaining function blocks and route the entire design. In this way, the engineer performs a placement of critical functions and the place-and-route software does not have as many constraints and does not need to consider as many possibilities. This makes the software run faster and gives it the capability to do more optimizations within these constraints.

The results of this type of floorplanning were, to be honest, terrible. First, an engineer does not have the ability to consider all of the myriad connections in a design. Although some functions may appear to need to be placed close to each other, doing so places them far from other blocks that may prove to be equally critical. As ASIC designs, and later FPGA and CPLD designs, grew larger, the ability for an engineer to instinctively know how to constrain layouts became even worse. And with less than ideal placements, the software had difficulty working within these constraints. In the meantime, software algorithms got better and computing power increased so that the place and route software could do a much better job than the engineer. The method of floorplanning simply did not work.

Recently, though, some changes have made floorplanning useful in some real, but limited, ways. Chip designs have now grown so large that the software to perform a complete place and route can take an extremely long time to find optimal results, even despite the increasing computational power available. Because of this, for large designs it can make sense to perform an initial placement of very large functional blocks (but not small functional blocks). The place and route software can then optimize the design within the blocks, creating a usable design in a reasonable amount of time.

- Built-in self-test (BIST) tools automatically create logic in your chip that enables it to test itself while it is in a system to determine that it is still functioning correctly.

- Static timing analysis software checks the timing numbers for your design and verifies that it will operate at the specified clock frequency or flags any paths that do not meet your timing requirements.

- Formal verification tools allow you to mathematically verify the functionality of a design and verify that two design descriptions are functionally equivalent.

- Place and route tools take the synthesized design description, determine how to optimally place the logic in the programmable device, how to optimally connect the logic together, and then create the bits used to program the device to implement your design.

- Floorplanning tools allow you to manually place high level blocks of logic in order to help the place and route tools finish faster.

- Programming tools create a bit pattern for the programmable device and load it into the device so that it implements your design.

Exercises

1. A testbench generator
   (a) Builds you a bench to sit on while testing your design.
   (b) Generates a benchmark test to compare different programmable devices.
   (c) Generates simulation tests for your design from your high level description of the test.
   (d) Tests assertions about the design.

2. An in situ tool
   (a) Allows a simulated device to communicate with another simulated device.
   (b) Allows a simulated device to communicate with a prototype device.
   (c) Allows a simulated, emulated, or prototype device to connect to a system and communicate in real time.
   (d) Allows a system to be simulated in real time.

3. Synthesis software
   (a) Converts a low level design description to a functionally equivalent high level description.
   (b) Converts a design in one HDL to an equivalent design in another HDL.
   (c) Creates a set of test vectors from a design description.
   (d) Creates a low level design description from a functionally equivalent high level design description.

4. ATPG stands for
   (a) Automatic test pattern generation
   (b) Asynchronous test pattern generation
   (c) Automatic timing property generation
   (d) Autonomous time priority generation

5. BIST stands for
   (a) Bring in some toast
   (b) Build internal synchronous test
   (c) Built-in standard test
   (d) Built-in self-test

6. Static timing analysis tools
   (a) Simulate a design using real timing numbers.
   (b) Analyze a design for all worst-case timing and determine whether the design meets your timing requirements.
   (c) Analyze your schedule for designing a chip and determine whether it is realistic and which tasks will take longer than expected.
   (d) Determine the precise timing your design will have when it is placed and routed.

7. Place and route tools
   (a) Create the bits that are used to program the device to implement your design.
   (b) Place the logic for your design in the programmable device and connect that logic together.
   (c) Find you a nice home and a good way to get to work.
   (d) Both a and b.

8. Select TRUE or FALSE for the following statements:
   (a) TRUE or FALSE: Static timing analysis has replaced timing simulation for determining the timing numbers for FPGA designs.
   (b) TRUE or FALSE: Dynamic timing analysis is a technique that will soon replace static timing analysis.
   (c) TRUE or FALSE: Scan insertion software is used to insert boundary scan chains into an FPGA.
   (d) TRUE or FALSE: Formal verification is a mathematic method of assuring that a design meets its timing requirements.
   (e) TRUE or FALSE: Floorplanning software allows you to place large chunks of your design in specific locations on the chip.
   (f) TRUE or FALSE: SRAM-based FPGAs are programmed in the system.
   (g) TRUE or FALSE: Serial PROMs are often used to load a design into an SRAM-based FPGA.

Chapter 8

Today and the Future

In this final chapter, I discuss some of the newer architectures and technologies that are becoming available or are on the horizon. I give my opinions on which ones are interesting and which aren't, which are overhyped and which are underhyped, and which will succeed and which won't.

Objectives

- Understand the newer devices that are becoming available or will be available in the future.

- Learn how these new technologies and design concepts relate to current designs

8.1 Cores

By a "core" I mean the basic functionality, excluding any extraneous circuits such as I/O buffers, that is found on a processor chip. There are two types of cores: soft cores and hard cores. The soft core, known as an IP core, is described by its logic function rather than by any physical implementation. Soft cores usually delivered to the customer as HDL code, which is then synthesized as part of the customer's design. Hard cores, on the other hand, consist of physical implementations of a function. With respect to CPLDs and FPGAs, these hard cores

165

are known as embedded cores because they are physically embedded onto the die and surrounded by programmable logic.

Many of the FPGA and CPLD vendors have begun offering cores. As the density of programmable devices increases, these cores allow engineers to create what is called a system on a programmable chip (SOPC) using a programmable device. In other words, whereas programmable devices were initially developed to replace glue logic, engineers can now place entire systems on a single programmable device. Systems consist of all kinds of complicated devices like processors. In order to place these complex functions within a programmable device, there are three options: Design the function yourself, purchase the HDL code for the function and incorporate it into your HDL code, or get the vendor to include the function as a cell in the programmable device. The second option is the IP core; the third option is the embedded core.

8.1.1   IP Cores

IP cores are often sold by third-party vendors that specialize in creating these functions. Recently, CPLD and FPGA vendors have begun offering their own soft cores. IP cores reduce the time and manpower requirements for the FPGA designer. IP cores have already been designed, characterized, and verified. Also, IP cores are often modifiable, meaning that you can add or subtract functionality to suit your needs.

But IP cores may also be expensive in terms of chip resources. IP cores can be optimized to a certain degree, but the complete optimization depends on its use in a particular device and also depends on the logic to which it is connected. IP purchased from a third party may not be optimized for a particular CPLD or FPGA vendor. Because of that, you may not be able to meet your speed or power requirements, especially after you have placed and routed it.

8.1.2   Embedded Cores

The embedded core is in many ways ideal for users, which is one reason why programmable device vendors are now offering embedded cores in their devices. The embedded core is optimized for the vendor's process, so that it achieves good timing and power consumption numbers. The embedded function is placed as a single cell on the silicon die, so its performance does not depend on the rest of your design because it will not need to be placed and routed.

Some embedded cores are analog devices that cannot be designed into an ordinary CPLD or FPGA. By integrating these functions into the device, you can avoid the difficult process of designing analog devices, and save the chips and components that would otherwise be required outside the programmable device.

Of course, there is a drawback to embedded cores. By using an embedded core in your programmable device, you tie the design to a single vendor. Unless another vendor offers the same embedded core, which is unlikely, switching to another vendor will require a large effort and will not be pleasant.

Another reason for offering embedded cores is a business reason. There are essentially two major players in the CPLD and FPGA markets: Xilinx and Altera. The smaller players have tried for years to compete with the result, generally, that their market share has remained flat or shrunk. In order for the smaller vendors to differentiate themselves from the big two, they need to find a niche market that they can dominate. These niche markets support those designs that need a very specific function. I should say that these niche markets may turn out to be very big. However, it is a bet-the-house risk, especially for the smaller companies. If a small company puts a lot of resources into developing and marketing a programmable device which includes a specific processor that ends up being designed into every personal computer, then it was a good bet. But if the vendor bets on the wrong processor, they could lose a huge amount of R&D money and get little revenue in return. This isn't as big a risk for the large vendors because they have more resources, more sales channels, and more cash to quickly change directions and develop new families of devices.

8.1.3   Processor Cores

Processor cores are commonly available as IP cores or embedded cores. These processors tend to be those that are designed for embedded systems because, almost by definition, programmable devices are embedded systems.

If the processor core is embedded, you will be using a processor that has been optimized and has predictable timing and power consumption numbers. For both types of core, software development tools are readily available. Off-the-shelf cross compilers and simulators can be used to debug code before the design has been completed and the programmable device is available.

An example of an FPGA with an embedded processor, along with other embedded cores, is shown in Figure 8.1.

8.1.4   DSP Cores

Digital signal processors (DSPs) are also commonly available as an IP core or an embedded core. DSPs are specialized processors used for manipulating sampled analog signals. DSPs are commonly used for audio and video filtering and compression. Many engineers have argued that as general processors become faster, DSPs will be less useful because the same functions can be accomplished on the generic processors. However, video and audio digitization, compression, and filtering requirements have increased in recent years as millions of users connect to

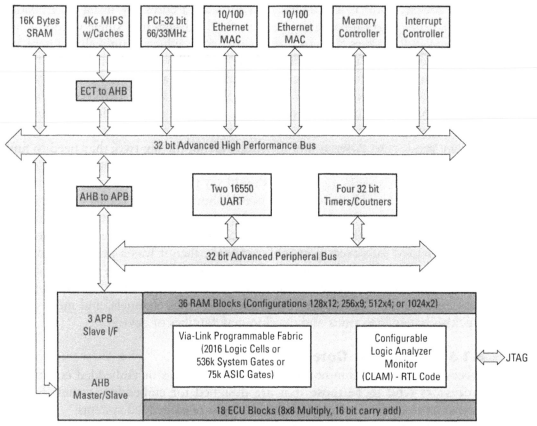

Figure 8.1   FPGA with embedded processor core (courtesy of Quicklogic Corporation)

the Internet and regularly upload and download all kinds of information over relatively limited bandwidth connections. So far, DSP demand for use in networking and graphics devices has been increasing, not decreasing.

8.1.5   Embedded PHY Cores

PHY cores are the analog circuitry that drives networks. Many companies are now integrating this functionality onto their devices. Because these devices include specialized analog circuitry, they are available only as embedded cores.

In the late nineties, during the heyday of the Internet, networking companies were springing up all over. In order to save design time, these companies could use FPGAs with PHY cores built in. Unfortunately, this boom didn't last, and some networking technologies did not find the mass acceptance that was predicted. For engineers designing an interface to a specific type of network, an FPGA with the appropriate PHY core can be a very good resource. For pro-

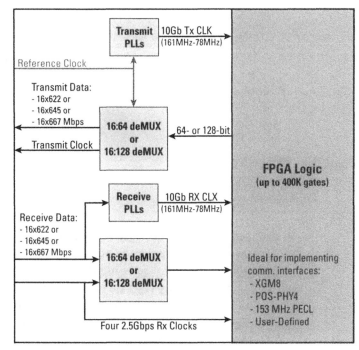

Figure 8.2   FPGA with embedded PHY core (copyright 2002 by Lattice Semiconductor Corporation)

grammable device vendors, it can be something of a risk to support a particular PHY core that may not end up being the standard that they expect or have the mass market acceptance that they are counting on.

Figure 8.2 shows an example of an FPGA with an embedded PHY core that can be programmed to interface to a variety of different networks.

8.2 Special I/O Drivers

Special I/O drivers are now being embedded into programmable devices. The newer buses inside personal computers need special high-drive, impedance matched drive circuits and input circuits with very specific voltage threshold values. Many vendors now offer programmable devices with I/O that meet these special requirements. Many times, these devices are the only way to design a programmable device that can interface with these buses.

8.3 New Architectures

Vendors are developing new architectures for CPLDs and FPGAs. Some vendors still make occasional attempts to create a fine-grained architecture where the logic blocks consist of small logic functions. Most of these attempts, I believe,

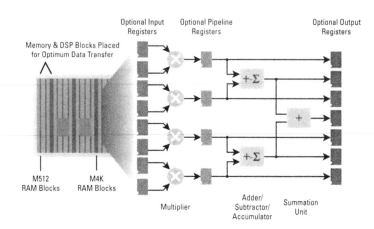

Figure 8.3   DSP core cell in an
FPGA (courtesy of Altera
Corporation)

are doomed to failure because routing is still the main constraint in any FPGA. Fine-grained architectures require more routing than large-grained architectures.

One type of architecture being developed has a logic block based on a DSP, as seen in Figure 8.3. This type of FPGA will be better for use in chips that need a significant amount of signal processing. I have certain doubts about this future path, though. First, the majority of programmable devices do not perform any DSP, so this architecture targets a relatively small market. Second, special tools will be needed to convert digital signaling algorithms for use in such a specialized FPGA. These tools will need to optimize the algorithm very well so that the FPGA realization can actually perform better than a standard DSP, or a generic processor, running code that has been optimized using tools and compilers that have been available for years.

8.4 ASICs with Embedded FPGA Cells

A relatively new concept is to embed FPGAs into ASICs. Vendors are approaching this embedded logic two different ways. One way is to create small programmable cells of logic that can be used in an ASIC. These cells are similar to the configurable logic blocks of an FPGA, and vendors could place them, along with hard logic cells, anywhere on an ASIC. The other way is to embed an FPGA core into an ASIC and allow logic to be placed around this core.

The technology of providing FPGA cells for ASIC designs is an interesting one. I don't have a good feel for the size of this market, though I feel that a market definitely exists. I see potential in several specific areas:

- Cost reduction. For engineers who are already designing systems that include both ASICs and FPGAs, putting FPGA cells inside the ASIC combines multiple chips into one hybrid chip. This will result in a significant cost savings by eliminating chips. For engineers who are considering a design that includes ASIC technology and FPGA technology, this solution saves PC board space, and the resulting hybrid chip will generally require fewer external pins because the ASIC/FPGA interface is now inside the chip. Smaller PC boards results in lower cost. More importantly, lower pin count on a chip results in significantly lower costs because package size is a large percentage of the overall per-piece cost of an ASIC.

- Changing communication protocols. We've already seen manufacturers use flash memory technology extensively in modem designs so that they could release modems before a communication protocol was finalized. This gave modem manufacturers that used this technology a head start in the market. When the protocol was finalized, the user simply needed to update the modem firmware. Manufacturers can use this technology in switches and routers and other complicated communication devices in the same way. Network device manufacturers can ship devices before a protocol is fully defined. Of course, they can do that now using discrete FPGAs in their design, but this technology offers cost advantages by placing all logic, both fixed and flexible, onto a single chip.

- Bus interfaces and memory interfaces. These are other areas that are good candidates for this technology. The FPGA functionality allows the engineer to fine tune the logic while it is in the field. I believe that the opportunity for this kind of market exists for very new interfaces that may not be well defined or for which accurate simulation models don't yet exist. However, I also believe that accurate simulation models exist for older, well-defined interfaces, so the technology will not be applied as much for supporting these legacy interfaces.

- Architecture enhancements. One interesting idea that this technology further enables is the ability to make architectural changes after a product has been manufactured and shipped. In my experience, manufacturers perform very little analysis of complex equipment to locate performance bottlenecks. This technology enables manufacturers to test changes to a system's architecture in the field. They can then incorporate those changes that resulted in better operation into the design. Also, different uses of a device may require different designs. Manufacturers can customize a device for particular customers based on the customer's environment and requirements.

- Reconfigurable computing. The concept of using FPGA devices to perform some of the algorithmic work of a general-purpose computer has excited researchers for several years. Currently, the work is mostly confined to universities and R&D labs because of the complexity and challenges from the

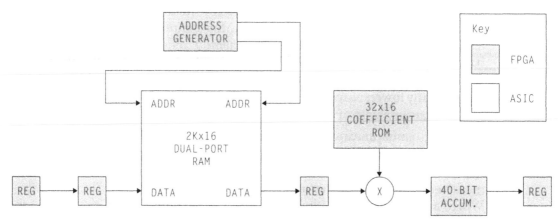

Figure 8.4   Mixed ASIC/FPGA design (copyright 2002, by Leopard Logic Corporation)

design of the software and the hardware. In particular, it has been difficult to develop compilers or interpreters that can take general algorithms, written in general programming languages like C, and map the functionality onto reconfigurable hardware. If researchers can resolve these issues, and reconfigurable computing becomes successful, this technology could be an ideal platform for it because it enables the tight integration of high-speed logic and reconfigurable logic on the same chip.

The example in Figure 8.4 shows a block diagram of an implementation of a 32-tap FIR filter. The shaded blocks are implemented in FPGA cells; the unshaded blocks are implemented in ASIC cells. The RAM is much easier to implement, and more efficient to implement, as a RAM cell than in an FPGA. By implementing the address generator and ROM in FPGA cells, the algorithm can easily be reprogrammed.

8.5 Summary

The latest programmable devices and future programmable devices hold great promise for smaller chip designs, cost reductions, and increased flexibility. I've given you my opinions about these devices. I may turn out to be wrong. Things may change and by the time you read this, you may be seeing devices I haven't even predicted yet. "Core" technology, special I/O drivers, new architectures, and ASICs embedded with FPGA cells all offer potential improvements in FPGA and CPLD design. I can only leave you with the immortal words of the amazing and mysterious Criswell from that unforgettable film, *Plan Nine From Outer Space*, "We are all interested in the future, for that is where you and I are going to spend the rest of our lives."

Appendix A

Answer Key

Chapter 1, "Prehistory: Programmable Logic to ASICs"

1. What does the term ASIC mean?

    (c) Application Specific Integrated Circuit

2. Each programmable device is matched with its description in the following table.

    a. PROM   (A) A memory device that can be programmed once and read many times.

    b. PLA   (D) A logic device with a large AND plane and a large OR plane for implementing different combinations of Boolean logic.

    c. PAL   (E) A logic device with a large AND plane and a small, fixed number of OR gates for implementing Boolean logic and state machines.

    d. CPLD   (C) A logic device that is made up of many PAL devices.

    e. FPGA   (B) A logic device that can be used to design large functions like an ASIC except that it can be programmed quickly and inexpensively.

3. Listed is the correct device for each statement — PALs or ASICs.

    (a) PALs have a short lead-time.

    (b) ASICs are high-density devices.

    (c) ASICs can implement very complex functions.

    (d) PALs do not have NRE charges.

    (e) PALs are programmable.

Chapter 2, "Complex Programmable Logic Devices (CPLDs)"

1. What does the term CPLD mean?

    (a) Complex Programmable Logic Device

2. These are all of the parts of a typical CPLD.

    (a) I/O Block

    (d) Function Block

    (e) Interconnect Matrix

3. Which technology is not used for CPLD programmable elements?

    (d) DRAM

4. Which is not a characteristic of clock drivers

    (c) Low power

5. The layout of traces that connects a clock driver to the flip-flops in a CPLD is called

    (a) A clock tree

6. One advantage of the CPLD switch matrix routing scheme is that delays through the chip are

    (b) Deterministic

7. Embedded devices are (select one)

    (b) Devices that are embedded inside a CPLD

Chapter 3, "Field Programmable Gate Arrays (FPGAs)"

1. What does the term FPGA mean?

   (b) Field Programmable Gate Array

2. Here are all of the parts of a typical FPGA architecture.

   (a) Configurable Logic Blocks

   (c) Programmable Interconnect

   (d) Configurable I/O Blocks

3. TRUE or FALSE is selected for the following statements.

   (a) TRUE: Configurable I/O Blocks contain flip-flops on the inputs to enable a designer to reduce the hold-time requirement for the inputs.

   (b) TRUE: Configurable I/O Blocks contain flip-flops on the outputs to enable the designer to decrease the clock-to-output times of the outputs.

   (c) FALSE: FPGA programmable interconnect consists of lines that start at one end of the chip and continue to the other end to enable all CLBs to be connected.

   (d) TRUE: Programmable switches inside the chip allow the connection of CLBs to interconnect lines

   (e) TRUE: Programmable switches inside the chip allow the connection of interconnect lines to each other and to the switch matrix.

   (f) FALSE: Each flip-flop in an FPGA has its own unique clock line and clock buffer to reduce skew.

   (g) FALSE: Any input to an FPGA can be used for the clock input.

   (h) FALSE: Antifuse FPGAs use an industry standard process.

   (i) TRUE: Antifuse technology is faster than SRAM technology, in theory.

   (j) TRUE: SRAM FPGAs are more common than antifuse FPGAs.

4. These are all potential advantages of embedded devices

   (a) Reduced board area

   (b) Reduced power consumption

   (c) Reduced cost

   (d) Increased system speed

   (e) You don't need to design and test the embedded device

5. TRUE or FALSE is selected for each of the following statements about SRAM-based FPGAs and antifuse FPGAs.
   (a) TRUE: SRAM-based FPGAs are based on an industry standard technology
   (b) TRUE: In theory, SRAM-based FPGAs are much slower than antifuse FPGAs.
   (c) TRUE: Antifuse FPGAs retain their programming after being powered off and then on again.
   (d) FALSE: Antifuse FPGAs can be erased and reprogrammed.
   (e) TRUE: SRAM-based FPGAs can be erased and reprogrammed.
   (f) FALSE: In practice, SRAM-based FPGAs are much slower than antifuse FPGAs.
   (g) FALSE: SRAM-based FPGAs are programmed using high voltages.
   (h) TRUE: Antifuse FPGAs are programmed using high voltages.

6. Clock trees are designed for (select one)
   (c) Small delay and low skew

7. The following table shows the correct attributes of CPLDs and FPGAs.

	CPLD	FPGA
Architecture	PAL-like	Gate Array-like
Density	Low to medium	Medium to high
Speed	Fast and predictable	Application dependent
Interconnect	Crossbar	Routing
Power consumption	High per gate	Low per gate

Chapter 4, "Universal Design Methodology for Programmable Devices"

1. The three major goals of UDM-PD are
   (a) Design the device efficiently
   (d) Design a device that works reliably over the lifetime of the device
   (f) Plan the design efficiently

2. UDM is a methodology to design a device that
   (a) Is free from manufacturing defects
   (c) Functions correctly in your system
   (d) Works reliably over the lifetime of the device

3. UDM is a methodology to design a device efficiently, meaning
   (a) In the least amount of time
   (b) Using the least number of people
   (c) Using the least amount of resources

4. UDM is a methodology to plan a design efficiently, meaning
   (b) Knowing all necessary resources up front and allocating them as early in the process as possible
   (c) Creating a reasonable schedule as early in the process as possible

5. Here is the design flow with each phase in the correct order.
   (c) Write a specification
   (e) Specification review
   (g) Choose device and tools
   (k) Design
   (h) Simulate
   (j) Design review
   (l) Synthesis
   (i) Place and route
   (f) Resimulation
   (d) Final review
   (b System integration and test
   (a) Ship product!

6. A design specification should include the following:
   (b) A description of the I/O pins including output drive capabilities and input threshold levels
   (c) The estimated gate count
   (d) The target power consumption
   (e) Test procedures, including in-system test requirements
   (f) An external block diagram showing how the FPGA fits into the system
   (h) An internal block diagram showing each major functional section
   (i) Timing estimates, including setup and hold times for input pins, propagation times for output pins, and the clock cycle time
   (j) The target price
   (k) The package type

Chapter 5, "Design Techniques, Rules, and Guidelines"

1. The term HDL stands for
    (a) Hardware description language

2. The model levels on the left are matched with the correct description on the right.

(a) Algorithmic	A Describes a design in terms of mathematical functionality.
(b) Architectural	D Describes a design in terms of functional blocks.
(c) Register transfer level	E Describes a design in terms of Boolean logic and storage devices.
(d) Gate level	B Describes a design in terms of basic logic such as NANDs and NORs.
(e) Switch level	C Describes a design in terms of transistors and basic electronic components.

3. The following HDL levels are considered behavioral levels:
    (b) Algorithmic level
    (d) Architectural level

4. The following HDL levels are considered structural levels.
    (a) Switch level
    (c) Gate level
    (e) Register transfer level

5. These are all of the statements that are true about top-down design.
    (a) Allows better allocation of resources
    (b) Allows each small function to be simulated independently
    (c) Speeds up simulations
    (d) Facilitates behavioral modeling of the device
    (f) Allows a design to be split efficiently among the various team members

6. The five rules of synchronous design are
   (a) Data signals must go only to combinatorial logic or data inputs of flip-flops.
   (b) All data is passed through combinatorial logic and flip-flops that are synchronized to a single clock.
   (c) Clocks cannot be gated — in other words, clocks must go directly to the clock inputs of the flip-flops without going through any combinatorial logic.
   (h) No signal that is generated by combinatorial logic can be fed back to the same combinatorial logic without first going through a synchronizing flip-flop.
   (i) Delay is always controlled by flip-flops, not combinatorial logic.

7. The asynchronous circuits on the left have been matched with the equivalent synchronous circuits on the right.

   (a)   C
   (b)   D
   (c)   A
   (d)   B

8. TRUE or FALSE is selected for the following statements.
   (a) FALSE: Synchronizing flip-flops are used to eliminate metastability.
   (b) TRUE: In theory, a device can remain metastable forever.
   (c) TRUE: The chances of a device going metastable increases with higher clock frequencies.
   (d) FALSE: The chances of a device going metastable decreases with higher input voltage thresholds.
   (e) FALSE: Schmidt trigger inputs with hysteresis can eliminate metastability.
   (f) FALSE: Metastability is caused by faulty circuits.
   (g) TRUE: Metastability is caused by asynchronous signals coming into synchronous circuits.

9. These are all allowable uses of asynchronous logic.
   (a) To latch inputs from and outputs to an asynchronous bus as long as the signals are synchronized for use inside the design.
   (c) Asynchronous reset if it is done according to specific rules.

10. TRUE or FALSE is selected for the following statements.
    (a) TRUE: Floating buses can create signal noise.
    (b) TRUE: Floating buses can cause extra power consumption.
    (c) TRUE: Floating buses should be avoided in your design.

11. The following circuits avoid floating buses.
    Circuits a, b, and c all avoid floating buses.

12. TRUE or FALSE is selected for the following statements.
    (a) TRUE: Bus contention can reduce the reliability of your design over its lifetime.
    (b) TRUE: Bus contention should be minimized if it can't be eliminated entirely.

13. Circuit b has the greatest potential for bus contention because nothing prevents both drivers from being turned on at the same time.

14. Testability should be considered
    (a) At the beginning of the design effort.

15. How many internal nodes in a design should be observable?
    (d) As many as possible

16. Which one of these statements is true?
    (c) Scan chain insertion effectively turns a sequential design into a combinatorial design for testing purposes.

17. Which of the following structures is not required for BIST?
    (c) Linear feedback shift register (LFSR)

18. The 10/10 rule of testing is:
    (c) Testing circuitry should not up take more than 10 percent of the total circuitry and should not require more than 10 percent of the design and debug time.

Chapter 6, "Verification"

1. What is meant by the term "functional simulation?"
    (a) Simulating how a design functions, without regard to timing

2. What is meant by the term "toggle coverage?"

   (b) The number of nodes in a design that change state from 0 to 1 and from 1 to 0 during simulation as a percentage of the total number of possible state transitions.

3. What is meant by the term "code coverage?"

   (c) The percentage of code statements in a design that have been executed during simulation in every possible manner.

4. What is meant by the term "timing simulation?"

   (b) A simulation that includes timing delays.

5. Why is timing simulation typically no longer done for a design?

   (c) Static timing analysis is a faster, more exhaustive analysis of whether a design meets its timing requirements.

6. What is meant by the term "static timing analysis?"

   (a) A process that looks at a synchronous design and determines the highest operating frequency that does not violate any setup and hold-times.

7. What are the two types of formal verification?

   (a) Functional verification and equivalency checking.

Chapter 7, "Electronic Design Automation Tools"

1. A testbench generator

   (c) Generates simulation tests for your design from your high level description of the test.

2. An in situ tool

   (c) Allows a simulated, emulated, or prototype device to connect to a system and communicate in real time.

3. Synthesis software

   (d) Creates a low level design description from a functionally equivalent high level design description.

4. ATPG stands for

   (a) Automatic test pattern generation

5. BIST stands for

   (d) Built-in self-test

6. Static timing analysis tools

   (b) Analyze a design for all worst-case timing and determine whether the design meets your timing requirements.

7. Place and route tools

   (d) Both a and b (Create the bits that are used to program the device to implement your design; and place the logic for your design in the programmable device and connect that logic together)

8. TRUE or FALSE is given for the following statements:

   (a) TRUE: Static timing analysis has replaced timing simulation for determining the timing numbers for FPGA designs.

   (b) FALSE: Dynamic timing analysis is a technique that will soon replace static timing analysis.

   (c) FALSE: Scan insertion software is used to insert boundary scan chains into an FPGA.

   (d) FALSE: Formal verification is a mathematic method of assuring that a design meets its timing requirements.

   (e) TRUE: Floorplanning software allows you to place large chunks of your design in specific locations on the chip.

   (f) TRUE: SRAM-based FPGAs are programmed in the system.

   (g) TRUE: Serial PROMs are often used to load a design into an SRAM-based FPGA.

Appendix B

Verilog Code for Schematics in Chapter 5

Listing B.1   Figure 5.2

```
/*************************************************************/
// MODULE:        asynchronous race condition
//
// FILE NAME:     arace.v
// VERSION:       1.0
// DATE:          June 1, 2002
// AUTHOR:        Bob Zeidman, Zeidman Consulting
//
// CODE TYPE:     RTL
//
// DESCRIPTION:   This module defines a circuit with an
// asynchronous race condition. Note that this circuit
// will simulate fine, but a synthesis program won't know
```

Listing B.1   Figure 5.2 (Continued)

```
// how to synthesize it into a synchronous circuit.
//
/**********************************************************/

// DEFINES

// TOP MODULE
module arace(
     sig1,
     sig2,
     out);

// PARAMETERS

// INPUTS
input      sig1;      // data input
input      sig2;      // clock and clear input

// OUTPUTS
output     out;       // output

// INOUTS

// SIGNAL DECLARATIONS
wire       sig1;
wire       sig2;
reg        out;

// ASSIGN STATEMENTS

// MAIN CODE

// Reset condition
always @(negedge sig2) out <= 0;
```

Listing B.1   Figure 5.2 (Continued)

```
// Clocked condition
always @(posedge sig2) out <= sig1;


endmodule              // arace
```

Listing B.2   Figure 5.4

```
/***********************************************************/
// MODULE:      no race condition
//
// FILE NAME:   norace.v
// VERSION:     1.0
// DATE:        June 1, 2002
// AUTHOR:      Bob Zeidman, Zeidman Consulting
//
// CODE TYPE:   RTL
//
// DESCRIPTION: This module defines a circuit without an
// asynchronous race condition.
//
/***********************************************************/


// DEFINES

// TOP MODULE
module norace(
     clk,
     sig1,
     sig2,
     out);

// PARAMETERS

// INPUTS
input    clk;       // system clock
input    sig1;      // data input
input    sig2;      // clock and clear input
```

Listing B.2   **Figure 5.4 (Continued)**

```
// OUTPUTS
output      out;        // output

// INOUTS

// SIGNAL DECLARATIONS
wire        sig1;
wire        sig2;
reg         out;
reg         state;      // state variable

// ASSIGN STATEMENTS

// MAIN CODE

// Clocked condition
always @(posedge clk) begin
   state <= sig2;
   out <= (~state & sig1 & sig2) | (state & sig2 & out);
end

endmodule               // norace
```

Listing B.3   **Figure 5.5**

```
/************************************************************/
// MODULE:      delay dependent logic
//
// FILE NAME:   ddl.v
// VERSION:     1.0
// DATE:        June 1, 2002
// AUTHOR:      Bob Zeidman, Zeidman Consulting
//
// CODE TYPE:   RTL
//
```

Listing B.3   Figure 5.5 (Continued)

```
// DESCRIPTION:  This module defines a circuit that creates
// a pulse whose width depends on circuit delay.
//
/**********************************************************/


// DEFINES

// TOP MODULE
module ddl(
      a,
      z);

// PARAMETERS

// INPUTS
input      a;          // input

// OUTPUTS
output     z;          // output

// INOUTS

// SIGNAL DECLARATIONS
wire       a;
wire       a1;         // intermediate signal
wire       a2;         // intermediate signal
wire       a3;         // intermediate signal
wire       z;

// ASSIGN STATEMENTS
assign a1 = ~a;
assign a2 = ~a1;
assign a3 = ~a2;
assign z = a3 & a;
```

Listing B.3   Figure 5.5 (Continued)

```
// MAIN CODE

endmodule              // ddl
```

Listing B.4   Figure 5.6

```
/**********************************************************/
// MODULE:       synchronous delay logic
//
// FILE NAME:    sdl.v
// VERSION:      1.0
// DATE:         June 1, 2002
// AUTHOR:       Bob Zeidman, Zeidman Consulting
//
// CODE TYPE:    RTL
//
// DESCRIPTION:  This module defines a circuit that creates
// a pulse whose width depends on a clock signal.
//
/**********************************************************/

// DEFINES

// TOP MODULE
module sdl(
     clk,
     a,
     z);

// PARAMETERS

// INPUTS
input      clk;      // system clock
input      a;        // input
```

Listing B.4   Figure 5.6 (Continued)

```
// OUTPUTS
output       z:        // output

// INOUTS

// SIGNAL DECLARATIONS
wire         a:
reg          q:        // intermediate signal
wire         z:

// ASSIGN STATEMENTS
assign z = a & ~q:

// MAIN CODE

// Clocked condition
always @(posedge clk) q <= a:

endmodule              // sdl
```

Listing B.5   Figure 5.7

```
/*************************************************************/
// MODULE:       hold time violation
//
// FILE NAME:    hold.v
// VERSION:      1.0
// DATE:         June 1, 2002
// AUTHOR:       Bob Zeidman, Zeidman Consulting
//
// CODE TYPE:    RTL
//
// DESCRIPTION: This module defines a circuit that has
// a hold time violation.
```

Listing B.5   Figure 5.7 (Continued)

```
//
/***********************************************************/

// DEFINES

// TOP MODULE
module hold(
    clk,
    d1,
    d2,
    d4);

// PARAMETERS

// INPUTS
input       clk;        // system clock
input       d1;         // input
input       d2;         // input

// OUTPUTS
output      d4;         // output

// INOUTS

// SIGNAL DECLARATIONS
wire        clk;
wire        d1;
wire        d2;
reg         d3;         // intermediate signal
reg         d4;

// ASSIGN STATEMENTS

// MAIN CODE
```

Listing B.5   Figure 5.7 (Continued)

```
// Clocked condition
always @(posedge clk) d3 <= d1;

// Clocked condition
always @(posedge d3) d4 <= d2;

endmodule            // hold
```

Listing B.6   Figure 5.8

```
/************************************************************/
// MODULE:      no hold time violation
//
// FILE NAME:   no_hold.v
// VERSION:     1.0
// DATE:        June 1, 2002
// AUTHOR:      Bob Zeidman, Zeidman Consulting
//
// CODE TYPE:   RTL
//
// DESCRIPTION: This module defines a circuit that does
// not have a hold time violation.
//
/************************************************************/

// DEFINES

// TOP MODULE
module no_hold(
     clk,
     d1,
     d2,
     d4);

// PARAMETERS
```

Listing B.6   Figure 5.8 (Continued)

```verilog
// INPUTS
input     clk;       // system clock
input     d1;        // input
input     d2;        // input


// OUTPUTS
output    d4;        // output


// INOUTS


// SIGNAL DECLARATIONS
wire      clk;
wire      d1;
wire      d2;
reg       d3;        // intermediate signal
reg       d3d;       // intermediate signal
wire      d3p;       // intermediate signal
reg       d4;


// ASSIGN STATEMENTS
assign d3p = d3 & ~d3d;


// MAIN CODE


// Clocked condition
always @(posedge clk) begin
   d3 <= d1;
   d3d <= d3;
   if (d3p) d4 <= d2;
end


endmodule              // no_hold
```

Listing B.7   **Figure 5.9**

```
/*************************************************************/
// MODULE:       glitch
//
// FILE NAME:    glitch.v
// VERSION:      1.0
// DATE:         June 1, 2002
// AUTHOR:       Bob Zeidman, Zeidman Consulting
//
// CODE TYPE:    RTL
//
// DESCRIPTION:  This module defines a mux circuit with a
// potential glitch.
//
/*************************************************************/

// DEFINES

// TOP MODULE
module glitch(
     d0,
     d1,
     sel,
     z);

// PARAMETERS

// INPUTS
input     d0;          // data input
input     d1;          // data input
input     sel;         // select

// OUTPUTS
output    z;           // output
```

Listing B.7   Figure 5.9 (Continued)

```
// INOUTS

// SIGNAL DECLARATIONS
wire        d0;
wire        d1;
wire        sel;
wire        z;

// ASSIGN STATEMENTS
assign z = sel ? d1 : d0;

// MAIN CODE

endmodule              // glitch
```

Listing B.8   Figure 5.10

```
/**********************************************************/
// MODULE:       no glitch
//
// FILE NAME:    no_glitch.v
// VERSION:      1.0
// DATE:         June 1, 2002
// AUTHOR:       Bob Zeidman, Zeidman Consulting
//
// CODE TYPE:    RTL
//
// DESCRIPTION:  This module defines a mux circuit without a
// potential glitch.
//
/**********************************************************/

// DEFINES

// TOP MODULE
```

Listing B.8   Figure 5.10 (Continued)

```verilog
module no_glitch(
    clk,
    d0,
    d1,
    sel,
    z);

// PARAMETERS

// INPUTS
input       clk;        // system clock
input       d0;         // data input
input       d1;         // data input
input       sel;        // select

// OUTPUTS
output      z;          // output

// INOUTS

// SIGNAL DECLARATIONS
wire        d0;
wire        d1;
wire        sel;
wire        zp;         // intermediate signal
reg         z;

// ASSIGN STATEMENTS
assign zp = sel ? d1 : d0;

// MAIN CODE

// Clocked condition
always @(posedge clk) z <= zp;

endmodule               // no_glitch
```

Listing B.9   Figure 5.11

```
/**********************************************************/
// MODULE:      gated clock
//
// FILE NAME:   gated.v
// VERSION:     1.0
// DATE:        June 1, 2002
// AUTHOR:      Bob Zeidman, Zeidman Consulting
//
// CODE TYPE:   RTL
//
// DESCRIPTION: This module defines a circuit with a gated
// clock.
//
/**********************************************************/

// DEFINES

// TOP MODULE
module gated(
    clk,
    data,
    gate,
    out);

// PARAMETERS

// INPUTS
input       clk;        // system clock
input       data;       // data input
input       gate;       // gate input

// OUTPUTS
output      out;        // output

// INOUTS
```

Listing B.9   Figure 5.11 (Continued)

```
// SIGNAL DECLARATIONS
wire        clk;
wire        data;
wire        gate;
wire        gclk;        // gated clock
reg         out;

// ASSIGN STATEMENTS
assign gclk = gate & clk;

// MAIN CODE

// Clocked condition
always @(posedge gclk) out <= data;

endmodule                // gated
```

Listing B.10   Figure 5.12

```
/***********************************************************/
// MODULE:      not gated clock
//
// FILE NAME:   not_gated.v
// VERSION:     1.0
// DATE:        June 1, 2002
// AUTHOR:      Bob Zeidman, Zeidman Consulting
//
// CODE TYPE:   RTL
//
// DESCRIPTION: This module defines a circuit without a
// gated clock. This is an enable flip-flop.
//
/***********************************************************/

// DEFINES
```

Listing B.10   Figure 5.12 (Continued)

```verilog
// TOP MODULE
module not_gated(
    clk,
    data,
    gate,
    out);

// PARAMETERS

// INPUTS
input       clk;        // system clock
input       data;       // data input
input       gate;       // gate input

// OUTPUTS
output      out;        // output

// INOUTS

// SIGNAL DECLARATIONS
wire        clk;
wire        data;
wire        gate;
wire        mux;        // mux output
reg         out;

// ASSIGN STATEMENTS
assign mux = gate ? data : out;

// MAIN CODE

// Clocked condition
always @(posedge gclk) out <= mux;

endmodule                   // not_gated
```

Listing B.11   Figure 5.13

```
/***********************************************************/
// MODULE:      the enable flip-flop
//
// FILE NAME:   eff.v
// VERSION:     1.0
// DATE:        June 1, 2002
// AUTHOR:      Bob Zeidman, Zeidman Consulting
//
// CODE TYPE:   RTL
//
// DESCRIPTION: This module defines an enable flip-slop.
//
/***********************************************************/

// DEFINES

// TOP MODULE
module eff(
     clk,
     data,
     enable,
     out);

// PARAMETERS

// INPUTS
input      clk;        // system clock
input      data;       // input
input      enable;     // input

// OUTPUTS
output     out;        // output

// INOUTS
```

Listing B.11   Figure 5.13 (Continued)

```
// SIGNAL DECLARATIONS
wire        clk;
wire        data;
wire        enable;
reg         out;


// ASSIGN STATEMENTS


// MAIN CODE


// Clocked condition
always @(posedge clk) begin
   if (enable) out <= data;
end


endmodule               // eff
```

Listing B.12   Figure 5.15

```
/************************************************************/
// MODULE:      potentially metastable circuit
//
// FILE NAME:   meta.v
// VERSION:     1.0
// DATE:        June 1, 2002
// AUTHOR:      Bob Zeidman, Zeidman Consulting
//
// CODE TYPE:   RTL
//
// DESCRIPTION:  This module defines a circuit that can
// potentially go metastable due to an asynchronous input.
//
/************************************************************/


// DEFINES
```

Listing B.12   Figure 5.15 (Continued)

```verilog
// TOP MODULE
module meta(
    clk,
    async_in,
    out1,
    out2);

// PARAMETERS

// INPUTS
input       clk;        // system clock
input       async_in;   // asynchronous input

// OUTPUTS
output      out1;       // output 1
output      out2;       // output 2

// INOUTS

// SIGNAL DECLARATIONS
wire        clk;
wire        async_in;
reg         in;         // intermediate signal
reg         out1;
reg         out2;

// ASSIGN STATEMENTS

// MAIN CODE

// Clocked condition
always @(posedge gclk) begin
    in <= async_in;
    out1 <= in;
```

Listing B.12   Figure 5.15 (Continued)

```
    out2 <= in;
end

endmodule            // meta
```

Listing B.13   Figure 5.16

```
/*********************************************************/
// MODULE:      less metastable circuit
//
// FILE NAME:   less_meta.v
// VERSION:     1.0
// DATE:        June 1, 2002
// AUTHOR:      Bob Zeidman, Zeidman Consulting
//
// CODE TYPE:   RTL
//
// DESCRIPTION:  This module defines a circuit that can still
// potentially go metastable due to an asynchronous input.
// It uses a synchronizing flip-flop to lessen the chance
// of metastability.
//
/*********************************************************/

// DEFINES

// TOP MODULE
module less_meta(
    clk,
    async_in,
    out1,
    out2);

// PARAMETERS
```

Listing B.13   Figure 5.16 (Continued)

```verilog
// INPUTS
input       clk;            // system clock
input       async_in;       // asynchronous input

// OUTPUTS
output      out1;           // output 1
output      out2;           // output 2

// INOUTS

// SIGNAL DECLARATIONS
wire        clk;
wire        async_in;
reg         sync_in;        // synchronized input
reg         in;             // intermediate signal
reg         out1;
reg         out2;

// ASSIGN STATEMENTS

// MAIN CODE

// Clocked condition
always @(posedge clk) begin
   sync_in <= async_in;
   in <= sync_in;
   out1 <= in;
   out2 <= in;
end

endmodule                   // less_meta
```

Glossary

ABEL — An early hardware description language used to program PALs.

antifuse — Antifuses consist of microscopic structures, which, unlike a regular fuse, normally make no connection. A certain amount of current during programming of the device causes the two sides of the antifuse to connect.

architecture — A chip architecture refers to the high level structure of the chip.

asynchronous — An asynchronous design is any design that breaks a rule of synchronous design. An asynchronous design has delays that are not strictly controlled by a clock and therefore cannot be easily controlled and predicted.

ATM — Asynchronous Transfer Mode. A method of communicating network data at very high speeds.

BIST — Built-in self-test. This is a method of including test generation and monitoring circuitry in a chip design so that the chip can perform tests on itself to determine whether it is still working correctly.

Boolean Algebra — Invented by nineteenth century mathematician George Boole, this is an algebra that uses only the values 1 and 0. In 1939, Claude Shannon wrote his revolutionary Master's thesis *A Symbolic Analysis of Relay and Switching Circuits* that described for the first time how Boolean algebra could be applied to the design of computers.

boundary scan — Boundary scan uses the scan methodology but scans only nodes around the boundary of the chip, not internal nodes. This is effective for testing the FPGA's connections to the circuit board. It also uses much more refer resources (CLBs and routing) than full scan.

burn-in test — A burn-in test is one that is run for a large number of hours or days to stress the FPGA. Often, manufacturing problems where circuit parameters are marginal will not show up immediately, but will cause a failure after a short period of time.

CLB — Configurable logic blocks contain the logic for the FPGA. In a typical architecture, called a "large-grained" architecture, these CLBs will contain enough logic to create a small state machine. In a "fine-grained" architecture, more like a true gate array ASIC, the CLB will contain only very basic logic. All FPGAs available today have "large-grained" architectures.

CMOS — Complementary Metal Oxide Semiconductor — a common, low power, type of circuit for implementing logic functions in which the output is driven by two FET transistors.

code coverage — Code coverage measures the percentage of code statements in your design that have been executed during simulation in every possible manner.

combinatorial logic — This is the term for logic that implements Boolean equations and does not have any reliance on timing or sequencing.

contention — Contention occurs when two or more devices are driving the same wire at the same time.

core — The basic circuit of a specific function, excluding any extraneous circuits such as I/O buffers that would be found on a physical chip. For example, a processor core.

CPLD — Complex Programmable Logic Devices are chips that integrate a large number of PALs in a single chip, connected to each other through a cross-point switch.

CRC — Cyclic redundancy check — an error detecting technique used to ensure the accuracy of digital data transmissions. The transmitted messages are divided into predetermined lengths, called frames, and a special code is appended to the end of each frame. At the receiving end, the computer recalculates the expected code. If it does not match the transmitted code, an error is detected.

CUPL — An early hardware description language used to program PALs.

decay — Decay refers to the amount of time it takes for a signal to go from an unstable state to a stable one.

DeMorgan's Law — A law of Boolean Algebra that states that A & B = ~(~A | ~B) and that A | B = ~(~A & ~B). It was named after the nineteenth century mathematician Augustus De Morgan who discovered it.

DFT — Design for test — This is the practice of designing an FPGA with test circuitry included from the beginning.

DSP — Digital signal processor — a device that manipulates analog signals by converting them first to digital signals and then performing digital processes on them.

ECL — Emitter coupled logic — a common type of circuit for implementing logic functions that have very fast switching times.

EDA — Electronic design automation refers to tools for designing electronic devices.

EEPROM — Electrically erasable PROMs are read-only memories that can be programmed and erased using a higher voltage than that used in normal operation.

EPROM — Erasable PROMs are read-only memories that can be programmed with an electric current, but are erased using prolonged exposure to ultraviolet light.

equivalency checking — A type of formal verification that uses mathematical techniques to compare one design to another design to prove that they are equivalent. Thus if the first design is known to work correctly, the second design must also work correctly.

fine-grained architecture — Fine-grained FPGAs resemble ASIC gate arrays in that the CLBs contain only small, very

basic elements such as NAND gates, NOR gates, etc.

flash EPROM — Flash EPROM can be electrically programmed. Large sections can then be electrically erased very quickly. These memories have very fast access times compared to other types of PROMs, which are very slow.

floating — A floating signal is one that is not being actively driven to a logic 1 or logic 0.

formal verification — A mathematical technique for checking the functionality of a design. There are two types of formal verification: equivalency checking and functional verification.

FPGA — Field Programmable Gate Arrays are programmable chips that are structured very much like a gate array ASIC.

full scan — Full scan involves linking each flip-flop in a design into a scan chain. Sequences of values can then be scanned into and out of the chain in order to test the FPGA.

functional simulation — This term refers to simulating a design without considering actual timing numbers. This gives a good idea of whether the basic design is correct.

functional verification — A type of formal verification that uses formal mathematical techniques to prove that a condition (also called a property or assertion) can or cannot exist for a specific design.

glitch — An unexpected signal or short duration.

HDL — Hardware description language — these languages, such as Verilog and VHDL, are used to design a complex chip using programming language statements.

hold time — This is the amount of time that a signal on the input to a clocked device must be stable after a clock edge in order to guarantee that the clocked device will capture the correct value.

in-system programmability — The ability to reprogram a programmable device while it is soldered in a system and the system is powered up. SRAM-based devices can be programmed in-system. EPROM-, EEPROM-, and Flash PROM–based devices can be programmed in-system if the device includes the pins and internal circuitry to support this feature.

IP — Intellectual property — the parts of a chip design that are considered unique and are protected by patent laws. Usually this refers to a particular function that has been designed and tested and can be purchased to be used in another design. This type of IP does not have a physical implementation, but is typically represented by a hardware language description.

ISP — In-system programmability — the ability to reprogram a programmable device while it is in a system that is currently powered up and running.

JTAG — Joint Test Action Group — This term is commonly used to refer to the IEEE Standard 1149.1, which defines a specific form of boundary scan implementation. The name of the standard has come to be known by the name of the group that developed the standard, in the same way that the monster created by Dr. Frankenstein has come to be known by its creator's name.

large-grained architecture — In a large-grained FPGA, the CLB contains larger functionality logic. For example, it can contain two or more flip-flops and multiplexers and lookup tables (LUTs).

LUT — lookup table — the small SRAM in a CLB of an SRAM-based FPGA that is used to implement Boolean logic.

LVDS — low voltage differential signaling — a low noise, low power, low amplitude circuit for transmitting data at high-speeds.

macrofunction — A macrofunction, or macro, is simply a large, predefined, tested circuit that can be used freely in different FPGA designs.

metastability — Metastability refers to a state of an object that is stable, but any small disturbance to the object will cause it to leave the state. For example, a spoon lying on the floor is in a stable state. A spoon balanced on your nose is in a metastable state because any small disturbance will cause it to exit the current state and move into a stable state, on the floor. An asynchronous signal entering a synchronous circuit can cause the circuit to go into a metastable state, causing the circuit to become unpredictable.

Moore's Law — The original statement of this "law" in 1965 was that the number of transistors per integrated circuit double every couple of years. This "law" is really an observation that has held approximately true since 1965 when it was first stated by Gordon Moore, a founder, President, CEO, and Chairman of Intel Corporation. In order to remain accurate, people have modified the "law" from time to time to compensate for new observations. As of this writing, the "law" is that the number of integrated circuits per square inch doubles every 18 months.

mux — This is simply the short name for a multiplexer.

node — A node is the output of any gate in the design.

one-hot encoding — This is a method of designing state machines whereby each state is represented by a single flip-flop. This design method greatly reduces the combinatorial logic and uses more flip-flops than traditional state machine encoding, which makes more efficient use of the "large-grained" CLBs in an FPGA, which are the only kind of FPGAs currently available.

open drain — An output that can be driven to a low value or not driven at all. It cannot be driven to a high value.

PAL — Programmable arrays of logic are chips that are good for implementing state machines. Internally, like a PLA, they have large AND plane but a fixed size OR plane. In addition, there are often flip-flops and sometimes other logic such as XOR gates.

PALASM — An early hardware description language used to program PALs.

PECL — **Positive emitter coupled logic** — a common type of circuit for implementing logic functions. Similar to ECL, but the power supply for the logic is a positive voltage.

PLA — Programmable logic arrays are chips that are good for implementing combinatorial logic. Internally, they have a large number of inputs connected to an AND plane, the outputs of which go into a large OR plane.

place — This refers to placing logic inside CLBs of an FPGA in order to implement the FPGA design.

Plan Nine from Outer Space — The worst movie of all time, directed by Ed Wood, the worst director of all time. Highly recommended.

pragma — A message written into HDL code that tells the synthesis program to synthesize the design in some fashion that differs from the default method. For example, pragmas may alter the kinds of error messages that are generated or optimize the design in some way.

product terms — Terms in a Boolean equation that are ANDed together.

PROM — Programmable read only memory can be easily programmed with specific contents. Once programmed, the data cannot be erased.

pseudorandom — This refers to a sequence of numbers that are predictable and repeatable, but are produced in such a way that they have the same characteristics and distribution as numbers that are selected randomly.

race condition — A race condition occurs in an asynchronous circuit when the function is dependent on which of two signals get to a certain point first, and the winner of this race depends not on a controlled period of time, but the timing characteristics of the circuit.

regression testing — Successively running a set of simulation tests on a design that has been modified to determine that the modifications have not introduced new problems.

route — This refers to connecting CLBs and I/O blocks inside the FPGA, using the routing resources, to implement the FPGA design.

RTL — Register transfer level — this is a level of description using a hardware description language (HDL) that describes circuitry in terms of clocks, Boolean equations, and registers.

scan — Scan methodology involves creating scan chains from the flip-flops in a design so that sequences of values can be scanned into and out of the chain in order to test the FPGA.

scan chain — A scan chain is a structure where the output of each flip-flop in the chain is connected to the input of the next flip-flop in the chain. In this way, sequences of values can be scanned into and out of the chain in order to test the FPGA.

setup time — This refers to the amount of time before a clock edge that a signal must be stable on the input to a clocked device in order for the device to record the correct input value.

signature — The signature of an FPGA refers to the pattern that is expected to be output from the chip after a long deterministic sequence of inputs.

slew rate — The slew rate of a signal is a reference to how quickly it changes voltage.

SOPC — System on a programmable chip — this term is used to describe a very complex and very dense programmable device, a CPLD or FPGA, that can contain so much logic that it can be considered an entire system.

SRAM — Static random access memory is memory that can be written and read numerous times while in the system. It is very fast, and loses its data when it loses power.

static timing analysis — Static timing analysis is a process that looks at a synchronous design and determines the highest operating frequency of the design that does not violate any setup and hold times.

sum terms — Terms in a Boolean equation that are ORed together.

synchronous — Synchronous design adheres to the following rules:

- All data is passed through combinatorial logic, and through delay elements (typically flip-flops) that are synchronized to a single clock.
- Delay is always controlled by delay elements, not combinatorial logic.
- No signal that is generated by combinatorial logic can be fed back to the same combinatorial logic without first going through a synchronizing delay element.
- Clocks cannot be gated; clocks must go directly to the clock inputs of the delay elements without going through any combinatorial logic.
- Data signals must go only to combinatorial logic or data inputs of delay elements.

testbench — The simulation code that generates stimulus to a design and examines the outputs of the design.

threshold — The threshold of a gate is the voltage value or range of the input at which the output begins to change value.

timing simulation — Timing simulation involves including timing information in a functional simulation so that the real behavior of the chip is simulated. As a method of timing analysis, it is becoming less and less popular.

toggle coverage — When performing functional simulation, a rough estimate of the amount of simulation to perform is called toggle coverage, which measures the number of nodes in the FPGA that change state from 0 to 1 and from 1 to 0 during simulation as a percentage of the total number of possible state transitions (two per node because each node can change from 0 to 1 and from 1 to 0).

top-down design — Top-down design is the design method whereby high level functions are defined first and the lower level implementation details are filled in later.

TTL — Transistor-transistor logic — a common type of circuit for implementing logic functions in which the output is driven by two BJT transistors.

Verilog — A standard hardware description language, maintained by the Institute of Electrical and Electronic Engineers as IEEE-STD-1364.

VHDL — A standard hardware description language, maintained by the Institute of Electrical and Electronic Engineers as IEEE-STD-1076.

References

Logic Design Manual for ASICs. Santa Clara, CA: LSI Logic Corporation, 1989.

Davenport Jr., Wilbur B. *Probability and Random Processes.* New York, NY: McGraw-Hill Book Company, 1970.

Dorf, Richard C., editor. *Electrical Engineering Handbook.* Boca Raton, FL: CRC Press, Inc., 1993.

EDA Industry Working Groups Web site, `www.eda.org`

Maxfield, Clive "Max." *Designus Maximus Unleashed!* Woburn, MA: Butterworth-Heinemann, 1998.

Zeidman, Bob. *Introduction to Verilog.* Piscataway, NJ: Institute of Electrical and Electronic Engineers, 2000.

Zeidman, Bob. *Verilog Designer's Library.* Upper Saddle River, NJ: Prentice-Hall, Inc., 1999.

About the Author

Bob Zeidman is the president of Zeidman Consulting (www.ZeidmanConsulting.com), an EDA firm offering tools for simulating, prototyping, and emulating network devices. He is also the founder and president of The Chalkboard Network (www.chalknet.com), which provides seminars and courses on high tech topics via the Internet. Since the early eighties, Bob has designed integrated circuits and circuit boards and has written software for many different types of systems. As a consultant, his clients have included Apple Computer, Cisco Systems, Ikos Systems and Texas Instruments. Among his publications are technical papers on hardware and software design methods as well as two textbooks — *Verilog Designer's Library* published by Prentice-Hall and *Introduction to Verilog* published by IEEE Press. He has instructed courses at engineering conferences throughout the world. Bob earned bachelor's degrees in physics and electrical engineering at Cornell University and a master's degree in electrical engineering at Stanford University.

Index

TCP/IP Lean
Web Servers for Embedded Systems
Second Edition

by Jeremy Bentham

Implement dynamic Web programming techniques with this hands-on guide to TCP/IP networking. You get source code and fully-functional utilities for a simple TCP/IP stack that's efficient to use in embedded applications. This edition shows the Web server porting to the PIC16F877 chip as well as over an ethernet connection. Includes a demonstration port running on Microchip's PICDEM.Net demonstration board. CD-ROM included, 559pp, ISBN 1-57820-108-X, $59.95

MicroC/OS-II,
The Real-Time Kernel
Second Edition

by Jean J. Labrosse

Learn the inner workings of an RTOS! This release of MicroC/OS adds documentation for several important new features of the latest version of the software, including new real-time services, floating points, and coding conventions. It is a completely portable, ROMable, preemptive real-time kernel. Complete code is included for use in your own applications. Hardcover, CD-ROM included, 606pp, ISBN 1-57820-103-9, $74.95

Free shipping in the US & Canada from www.cmpbooks.com

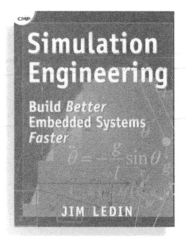

Simulation Engineering

by Jim Ledin

Learn when and how to use simulation methods. The entire range of important techniques are presented, beginning with the fundamentals of mathematical models, how to produce useful results, how to analyze the data and how to validate the models. Each chapter provides step-by-step instructions for developing a working simulation. Includes a review of state-of-the-art tools and administrative guidelines on management and communications. 303pp, ISBN 1-57820-080-6, $44.95

PPP for Embedded Systems

by John Bartas

Adapt PPP to stand-alone, embedded applications. You get details of the PPP protocol, C implementations of key algorithms, and a demonstration of a port to a commonly used microcontroller. Learn what kinds of special issues you may encounter in embedded systems implementations, as well as how the protocol will interact with other network components. 336pp, ISBN 1-57820-123-3, $39.95.

Free shipping in the US & Canada from www.cmpbooks.com

Printed and bound by CPI Group (UK) Ltd, Croydon, CR0 4YY

23/10/2024

01777685-0005